ROME'S
GREATEST EMPEROR:
VESPASIAN

ROME'S
GREATEST EMPEROR:
VESPASIAN

TONY SULLIVAN

PEN & SWORD **HISTORY**

AN IMPRINT OF PEN & SWORD BOOKS LTD.
YORKSHIRE – PHILADELPHIA

First published in Great Britain in 2024 by
PEN AND SWORD HISTORY
An imprint of
Pen & Sword Books Ltd
Yorkshire – Philadelphia

ISBN 978 1 03610 304 0

Typeset in Times New Roman 11.5/14 by SJmagic DESIGN SERVICES, India.
Printed and bound in the UK by CPI Group (UK) Ltd.

Pen & Sword Books Ltd includes the Imprints of Atlas, Archaeology,
Aviation, Discovery, Family History, Fiction, History, Maritime, Military,
Military Classics, Politics, Select, Airworld, Frontline Publishing, Leo
Cooper, Remember When, Seaforth Publishing, The Praetorian Press,
Wharncliffe Local History, Wharncliffe Transport, Wharncliffe True Crime
and White Owl.

For a complete list of Pen & Sword titles please contact
PEN & SWORD BOOKS LIMITED
George House, Units 12 & 13, Beevor Street, Off Pontefract Road,
Barnsley, South Yorkshire, S71 1HN, England
E-mail: enquiries@pen-and-sword.co.uk
Website: www.pen-and-sword.co.uk

or

PEN AND SWORD BOOKS
1950 Lawrence Rd, Havertown, PA 19083, USA
E-mail: uspen-and-sword@casematepublishers.com
Website: www.penandswordbooks.com

CONTENTS

TABLES

FIGURES

CLASSICAL SOURCES

CIL The *Corpus Inscriptionum Latinarum* collection of ancient Latin inscriptions.

RIB Roman inscriptions of Britain

Bellum Gallicum, The Gallic Wars, by Julius Caesar, 100-44 BC

Geographica, Geography, Strabo c. 64 BC- AD 24

Naturalis Historia, Natural History, Pliny the Elder, AD 23-79

Bellum Judaicum, The Jewish War, Titus Flavius Josephus, AD first century

De Vita Caesarum, The Lives of the Twelve Caesars, Suetonius AD 69-122

De vita Julii Agricolae, The Life of Agricola, Tacitus AD 56-120

De origine et situ Germanorum, On the Origin and Situation of the Germans, Tacitus AD 56-120

Historiae, Histories, Tacitus AD 56-120

Ab excessu divi Augusti, The Annals, Tacitus AD 56-120

De Munitionibus Castrorum, Concerning the fortifications of a military camp, unknown, 1st-2nd century

Ektaxis kata Alanon, The order of battle against the Alans, Lucius Flavius Arrianus (AD Second century)

Strategemata, Stratagems, Polyaenus AD 2nd century

Historia Romana, Roman History, by Cassius Dio c. AD 155-235

History of the Roman Empire since the Death of Marcus Aurelius by Herodian c. AD 170-240

Liber De Caesaribus, Life of the Caesars, Aurelius Victor, c. 320-390

Historia Augusta anonymous author, 4th century

Epitoma rei militaris, Concerning Military Matters, by Vegetius, 4th century

ACKNOWLEDGEMENTS

Many thanks to Zane Green and Alisa Vanlint of Legio Secunda Augusta and Ludus Augusta for providing some excellent images. Thanks to Owain Edwards of Castell Henllys Iron-Age Village, Wales for kind permission of photographs of re-enactment of first-century Briton and typical iron-age roundhouses.

INTRODUCTION

A lone warrior strained his eyes as he looked out from the southern shore across the sea. Beyond lay Gaul and, if rumours were true, an enemy was mustering. This enemy was no mere raiding party from a neighbouring tribe or from across the western sea. Spies and merchants had brought back stories of a huge fleet being built. Nearly a century had passed since the Romans had thrust northwards across the Alps and the tribes of Gaul had submitted or been conquered one by one. Now a large host of soldiers gathered and prepared, bent on taking the land and enslaving the people. The watchman remembered when similar stories circulated amongst his tribe just a few years before. How they had all laughed when they learned that the Emperor Caligula had marched his army north merely to collect sea-shells from the Gallic beaches. Was an invasion any more likely now that the Romans had a frail old man as their leader? What battles had this Claudius ever fought? How could the proud Britons be scared of such a man?

The warrior pulled his cloak around his bare chest. A single brooch clasped at his shoulder.

The cloak hid the swirling blue patterns of his tribe which adorned his body. Similar patterns marked a large oval shield slung across his back. His right hand held a long, broad-headed spear. He sat astride his mount, much smaller than modern horses, his feet hanging loosely against its flanks.

Our watchful-Briton might recall his grandfather's tales around the evening fire, telling stories about what *his* grandfather told him when the Romans last came. In those days the famous Julius Caesar had taken a great fleet across the narrow sea and was driven back by the Britons. Two summers in a row, he had come and twice the chariots had bitten at his ankles as they drove the Romans back into the sea. Songs and stories of such deeds were among the more popular entertainments. Yet wiser heads were not so dismissive. The Romans had conquered all of Gaul. Their armies were undefeated in the field. They did not fight like normal men but together as though of one mind, one huge beast made of flesh and iron. They reminded the younger warriors that, despite the legends, a great battle was lost. A tribal hill fort destroyed. Tribute was demanded and paid, for a time at least. Hostages were taken. Many had long predicted that the Romans would one day return.

The warrior turned his head from the direction of the Gallic coast and looked west. He narrowed his eyes and focused on a faint shape in the distance. Other dots appeared on the horizon. The leading dot grew larger until it turned into the unmistakeable shape of a ship. As his eyes adjusted, he realised that there were several ships hugging the coast heading east, towards his position. It took just five minutes for the lead ship to get close enough to confirm his fears. This was no mere trading vessel. The accompanying dots were now dozens and were followed by scores more appearing in the distance.

The *liburna bireme* was the most common warship used by the Romans in the first century. Two banks of thirty oars, sixty each side, keeping time with a rhythmic drumming. One hundred and twenty oarsmen heaved at their work. The principal weapon was a bronze or iron ram, designed to break the hulls of enemy ships and sink them. But these ships also had an array of deadly artillery. Ballistae capable of firing stones or bolts and onagers which threw larger stones to cripple an enemy ship. A ballista bolt could impale a man and stones caused horrific, crushing injuries.

If these deadly machines failed, the Romans could engage the *corvus*, an eleven-metre spiked boarding ramp, which, when alongside, smashed through the deck and held it fast. This allowed marines to swarm across and fight hand to hand. But there was no prospect of a naval engagement here. What would have been of more concern to a watching Briton were the hundreds of transport ships accompanying the warships. Many of these had been built by the northern Gallic and Germanic tribes such as the Veneti, Chauci and Frisi. Caesar described some of their boats in detail:[1] Flat-bottomed with high prows and sterns and oaken hulls. Foot-wide cross beams secured by nails as thick as a man's thumb. Anchors with iron chains and sails made from raw hides or leather.

Such a sight would have been awe-inspiring to the average Briton. Nine hundred ships stretched out along the coast. To put this into perspective William the Conqueror is believed to have used fewer than 800 ships in 1066. A few weeks before Harald Hardrada had invaded the north with 300 ships. The Spanish Armada of 1588 had approximately 130 ships. This was a fleet designed to take and hold new land.

The Briton looked on grimly as the fleet inched its way along the coast. He had seen enough. Turning his mount, he headed towards the tribe's stronghold, a day's ride inland. How would they take the news? Would they side with the Catuvellauni to the north? The younger warriors were eager to fight, but some of the elders advised that they make offers of peace and ally with the Atrebates and Regni, both friendly to Rome. An envoy from the brothers Caratacus and Togodumnus of the Catuvellauni argued persuasively for war. The memory of their ancestors demanded that they not bow their heads meekly to the Romans. Their Gallic brothers across the sea were now little more than slaves beneath the Roman heel. Our lone Briton, eager for glory, would fight, but how many of his brethren would join him?

As the warrior rode away a man on the lead ship scanned the coast. The Romans had half expected to see the cliffs lined with warriors as Julius Caesar described. The legionaries were trained and ready for the assault. The flat-bottomed ships would get as close as possible while the warships would rake the beach with missile fire. Ballistae would fire iron bolts and stone powerful enough to rip limbs and decapitate their victims. The Roman turned his head from the lone figure, dismissing him as a threat. Wherever he was going the Romans would find land before he could deliver the news in time.

He turned to the crew. Battle-hardened marines hauled at the oars. Sitting on the raised deck were a full century of legionaries from the Second Augusta. Eighty men, hand-picked, to defend the legion's eagle and commander. This man was Titus Flavius Vespasianus. His legion was to prove pivotal in the campaign ahead. Thirty-three years of age he was a strong, well-built man, with a rather strained expression that some would later mock. No one dared mock him here. Discipline was harsh and a man could be flogged for insolence.

Vespasian wore the regalia and clothing of a legionary legate. Under a fine quality muscled-cuirass was a short-sleeved tunic with a thick stripe denoting his senatorial rank. The tunic stopped just below the knees. As did a pair of short breeches, *bracae*. Good quality leather boots adorned his feet and a cloth band around his chest marked his rank. Strips of leather, *pteryges*, protected his hips and groin whilst smaller strips covered his shoulders. A red cloak, fastened by a single circular brooch on his right shoulder, kept out the morning chill. A gold ring marked his senatorial status, something that would have made his ambitious mother proud.

A reconstruction of the uniform of a first-century Roman legate can be seen in figure 1. In reality, Vespasian had a very different appearance than the man in the picture. We must imagine a much stockier, heavier-set man. Most of his busts portray him as emperor in his 60s so we can take the example in figure 2 and imagine the same man at the age of 33.

Little did anyone suspect, least of all Vespasian himself, that this man would one day be emperor. He had little reason to dream of such a destiny, having risen from a relatively obscure equestrian family.

Right: Figure 1: Uniform of a first-century legate. (Steven Cockings)

Below: Figure 2: Bust of Vespasian. (Wikimedia Commons)

In any event the Julio-Claudia dynasty seemed unassailable, even after the excesses of the unstable Caligula and his murder just two years before. In addition, Claudius had an heir, Tiberius Claudius Caesar (later known as Britannicus), although he was just two years old at the time. Vespasian's own son, Titus, was just four and the two boys would grow to become firm friends.

All this was in the future. Vespasian's mind may have occasionally turned to his first son and beloved home in the Sabine hills, north of Rome. But there was a job to do. On the deck of the bireme next to Vespasian was his elder brother Sabinus, who would fight alongside him in the coming campaign. Neither man could predict if it would lead to success and glory or ignominious defeat and death.

Not all Britons would have looked on in dread at the sight of this fleet. Many, such as the Atrebates and other southern tribes, welcomed the arrival of the Romans. They had no love for the more dominant Catuvellaunian residing north of the Thames. Trade had brought wealth and prosperity for many. Raiding by their northern neighbours had brought humiliation. Vengeance is a powerful motivation. Inter-tribal strife was endemic and would prove the Britons' undoing.

Yet the Romans knew this would be a hard fight. No Roman alive would have remembered Caesar's incursions over ninety years before. Four legions and as many auxiliaries were now packed into 900 ships and headed into the unknown. One wonders what thoughts went through Vespasian's head. They had all heard of the tales of Varus and the three legions lost in the Teutoburg Forest. No doubt Vespasian prayed to the gods that he would avoid that fate.

What awaited him and his men on the beach? Julius Caesar's Gallic Wars were well-known, and a well-educated senator would have been very familiar with the story. The cliffs lined with fearsome Britons. Tall, savage, covered in blue swirling patterns, they had nearly succeeded in driving even the great Caesar into the sea. Yet the Romans could see no sign of the Britons. The legionary legate knew this campaign could make or break his career. It could even prove fatal. But it was this campaign that propelled Vespasian on a road that would lead to fame and glory: a political career that would grant him a coveted term as a consul and governorship; a military reputation that would later cause Nero to turn to him to lead the reconquest of Judea, a decision that would place Vespasian at the head of a huge army just as the empire descended into the chaos of 'The Year of the Four Emperors'. Who was this man looking at the coast of Britain for the first time in AD 43?

Titus Flavius Vespasianus was born on 17 November AD 9 in the village of Falacrinae, north-east of Rome. He was the son of Titus Flavius Sabinus, a moneylender and tax collector, a member of the equestrian order, the second rank in Roman society. His mother was Vespasia Polla, daughter of a *praefectus castrorum*, a camp prefect. Her brother rose to the senatorial order, as did both her sons, Vespasian en route to the highest office of all. Vespasian was brought up and educated in the Tuscan countryside at Cosa by his paternal grandmother, Tertulla.

In the AD 30s he entered the senatorial order, rising up the *cursus honorum*. A *quaestor* (financial administrator and lowest and first rank on the *cursus honorum*), *aedile* (responsible for the maintenance of public buildings, infrastructure, public order and festivals) and *praetor* (elected magistrate and commander of an army). It was this position that led him to be placed in command of a legion, Legio II Augusta, in the invasion of Britain in 43 AD.

His career advanced under the Emperor Claudius and he was awarded the consulship in AD 51, the highest elected public position. He fell out of favour with the emperor's wife, Agrippina, and retired from public life. Eventually brought back by Agrippina's son, Nero, in AD 63, he was appointed governor of the Roman province of Africa. He fell from grace again when he fell asleep during one of Nero's musical recitals. However, shortly after he was appointed to suppress the Jewish revolt in AD 66, a bloody affair for which we have one of the most detailed contemporary accounts of both Vespasian and ancient warfare.

His success in Judea found him in an opportune position when Galba's rebellion caused Nero to commit suicide in 68. The Year of the Four Emperors was one of blood and treachery. Galba was murdered but his successor, Otho, was defeated by Vitellius and took his own life. Vespasian made his move and was declared emperor in the summer of 69. His troops entered Rome and bloody street fighting ensued, leaving thousands dead. Vitellius was dragged out of his hiding place and struck down on the Germonian Stairs, aptly nicknamed as 'The Stairs of Mourning'.

The start of Vespasian's reign was marked by the Batavian revolt, brutally repressed. Rome expanded its borders in Britain both west and north, a process that would eventually lead to General Agricola's dramatic victory at Mons Graupius in c. 83, a few years after Vespasian's death. The Jewish War rumbled on under Titus and saw the destruction of Jerusalem and siege of Masada.

Vespasian ruled nearly ten years, from 1 July 69 to 23 June 79. He was generally well regarded by contemporary and later writers as amiable, down to earth and witty. He was known for his patronage of the arts. Pliny the Elder dedicated his great work, *Natural History*, to Vespasian's son Titus. He was also remembered for his public works and buildings, most notably the *Amphitheatrum Flavium*, Flavian Amphitheatre, known today as the Colosseum.

He left behind two sons, Titus and Domitian, who followed him on the throne, forming the period known as the Flavian dynasty. Contemporary writers viewed them in a better light than the Julio-Claudian dynasty that preceded them, Tiberius, Caligula and Nero especially coming in for much criticism. The Flavians were followed by the 'Five Good Emperors': Nerva, Trajan, Hadrian, Antoninus Pius and Marcus Aurelius. But it is Vespasian whom contemporary and later historians credit for stabilising the empire and bringing peace after the upheavals that led to Nero's death.

The Roman Republic and Empire have proved a rich seam for film and TV producers as well as authors, both fiction and non-fiction. Classics such as *Ben Hur* (1959) with Charlton Heston; *Spartacus* (1960) with Kirk Douglas as the lead and *Cleopatra* (1963) starring Richard Burton and Elizabeth Taylor and, more recently, HBO's *Rome* series gave an entertaining and realistic portrayal of Caesar's rise to power. A significant number of films have also focused on Julius Caesar. Other common backdrops to films include the reign of Nero, destruction of Pompeii, the end of the Roman Empire and the rise of Christianity.

Perhaps surprisingly, few films or TV series have dealt with the Flavian dynasty. Aside from documentaries on the siege of Masada I could only find one fictionalised 1993 example, *Age of Treason*, set in Vespasian Rome. However, this omission may soon be rectified. An epic 'sword-and-sandal' television series began filming in 2023 with Anthony Hopkins starring as the Emperor Vespasian. Based on the 1958 book, *Those About to Die*, by Daniel Mannix, it has fans eagerly anticipating an experience to rival the 2000 favourite *Gladiator* directed by Ridley Scott and starring Russell Crowe.

One of my previous books, *The Real Gladiator: The True Story of Maximus Decimus Meridius*, covered the historical background to that film. Russell Crowe's character was of course fictional. However, there were two figures who closely resembled Maximus Decimus Meridius, although neither, as far as we know, were 'father to a murdered son, husband to a murdered wife', at least not in the context presented in the film. Like Vespasian, they both rose from the equestrian order to become senators.

The first was the general Marcus Valerius Maximianus who led the armies of Marcus Aurelius in the final battle of the second Marcomannic war. It is this battle that is dramatically portrayed in the opening scene of *Gladiator*. During an impressive military career he killed Valao, chieftain of Naristi, in single combat and received a stallion from the emperor as a reward. The second figure is Tiberius Claudius Pompeianus who rose to become the emperor's trusted general and was rewarded with the hand of his daughter Lucilla, played in the film by Connie Nielsen. Contrary to the film, Lucilla is recorded by contemporaries as despising her husband for his age (she was less than half his age at 19) and low rank (Lucilla was recently widowed by the death of Lucius Verus, co-emperor and adoptive brother to Marcus).

Like Vespasian, both men were from the equestrian order. All three rose to the rank of senator. One of the contemporaries of Maximianus and Pompeianus was another equestrian, Pertinax. Like Vespasian, he obtained the highest position of all. Yet his reign was cut short to only three months whilst Vespasian ruled for a decade.

In *Gladiator*, one theme that runs throughout is the idea that Marcus Aurelius wished to return the empire to its republican roots. This is pure fiction as he groomed his son Commodus for succession. Yet this nostalgia for republican virtues persisted. Another theme was a noble citizen taking responsibility to deal with an emergency but relinquishing power when the emergency is over. Thus, in the film Maximus is offered the throne by Marcus Aurelius and turns it down. In reality Pompeianus was also asked, not once but three times. Each time he declined, first after he married Lucilla, secondly by Pertinax after the death of Commodus and lastly by the doomed Didius Julianus as Severus Septimius advanced on Rome in AD 193.

The film was notable by the portrayal by Joaquin Phoenix of Commodus, the psychotic son of Marcus Aurelius, winning him a nomination for best supporting actor at the Academy Awards. One memorable scene has Maximus, reduced to fighting as a gladiator, singlehandedly killing several opponents in the arena before turning to the crowd and shouting, 'Are you not entertained?' The answer for the majority of cinema-goers and those watching at home was surely 'yes!'we were indeed entertained.

The question I addressed in my book was, would we be less entertained if the film had been more historically accurate? I argued that the actual history was in fact just as entertaining and dramatic as anything Hollywood could dream up. In the film, Commodus meets his death in a final dramatic fight with Maximus. Yet the true history sounds every bit as dramatic and it is worth comparing the historical record with the film's portrayal.

Commodus now planned some form of ceremony for the festival of Saturnalia in mid- to late-December. Shocked at the emperor's plan to fight in the arena as a common gladiator, his two chief advisors, Laetus, the praetorian prefect, and Eclectus, his steward, begged him not to debase his office. Angrily throwing them out he next turned on his former concubine Marcia. Retiring to bed drunk he fell asleep. It was only chance that caused a young slave boy to pick up the emperor's writing tablet and walk out of the room straight into Marcia. We can only wonder about her reaction on seeing a list of names for execution with her own at the top, alongside Laetus and Eclectus. The terrified three hatched a rushed plot. On the last day of AD 192 Commodus was poisoned. But he managed to vomit enough of it up to survive. No doubt suspicious he retired to his bath. Another panicked plot ensued. This time the emperor's wrestling partner was employed to finish him off. Commodus died naked, in the bath, strangled to death.

My book concluded that history was every bit as interesting and entertaining as fiction. The proposed series with Antony Hopkins is billed as an epic drama set during Vespasian's reign and focusing on the drama of gladiatorial contests. It will no doubt prove hugely successful. This book will look at the real history behind both Vespasian, first-century Rome and gladiatorial contests. Hopefully, it will be as entertaining as the forthcoming TV series whilst providing the historical background behind events.

Chapter 1

THE HISTORICAL
BACKGROUND

The foundation of Rome is shrouded in legend. What is clear is that in both the republic and imperial periods the Romans had a deep aversion to the concept of kingship. This was often at odds with the reality of centralised authority held by one man. Vespasian was born during the reign of the first of these imperators, Gaius Octavius, who later named himself Gaius Julius Caesar Octavianus. The senate awarded him the name *Imperator Caesar Augustus* and the name Augustus is how many remember him today. Vespasian reached adulthood during the reign of his successor, Tiberius. He managed to survive the murderous Caligula and rose to prominence under Claudius.

Whilst the Julio-Claudian dynasty appeared firmly established, Vespasian may have come across those with opposing sympathies. His own grandfather had fought for Pompey in the civil war against Julius Caesar. One wonders what his immediate family thought when Caesar was assassinated. A young man of 20 at the time would have been 73 when Vespasian was born. It is likely that, as a young man, he came into contact with people with republican leanings.

However, the change from the Republic to the Principate could be seen as an inevitable consequence of the expansion of Roman power across the Mediterranean. A small city state is a very different entity compared to a sprawling empire with powerful governors and generals able to consolidate power across a wide geographical area. Perhaps the only way to keep it together was a powerful centralised authority. Such was the world Vespasian was born into, an empire stretching from Egypt to the Atlantic coast; from the Rhine to northern Africa.

Vespasian was also raised in a society with a relatively rigid hierarchy. Despite this, a certain amount of social mobility was possible, amply demonstrated by his rise from equestrian status to the senate and, ultimately, to the highest office of all. A brief look at Rome's history will provide a backdrop to the world Vespasian was born into.

Early history

Roman tradition claimed the city was founded in 753 BC on seven hills overlooking the banks of the Tiber. It lay sixteen miles from the western coast of the Italian peninsula. A common foundation myth named the brothers Romulus and Remus as the founders of the city. A later legend made them the descendants of Aeneas, a Prince of Troy who escaped the destruction of the city at the hands of the Greeks, famously described in Homer's Iliad.

Here we will follow the tale as told by Livy c. 20 BC.[1] A little to the south of the future great city lay the town of Alba Longa in the Alban Hills. In this region a certain Numitor, descendant of Aeneas, ruled. Following a palace coup he was overthrown by his wicked brother, Amulius. Fearing possible future rivals, Amulius forced his niece, Numitor's daughter, Rhea Silvia, to become a priestess, a role that required chastity. One wonders why he didn't simply kill her but perhaps placing her in a temple made him look magnanimous.

Amulius no doubt felt secure thinking he had cleverly prevented the birth of any potential rivals. But his plan failed. Rhea was visited by the God of War himself, Mars. Mars was after only one thing and this time it wasn't war. Livy, though personally sceptical, tells that Rhea fell pregnant by Mars and twin boys duly arrived. The usurper Amulius was outraged and ordered the boys to be drowned. No scruples about the murder of relatives this time.

Servants were sent to perform this grisly task but, being more squeamish than their master, they are unable to go through with the murder of the helpless babes. Instead, they simply abandon the infants to their fate by the banks of the river. Luckily, a nurturing she-wolf comes across the brothers and her maternal instincts override any usual antipathy towards humans. She rescues the twins and suckles them. They are later found and raised by a kindly shepherd, Faustulus, and his wife, Acca Larentia. Livy attempts to rationalise the story, noting the Latin word for wolf, *Lupa*, was also a colloquial term for prostitute.[2]

his predecessor, and continued in the same vein against his political opponents. Among them were many senators.

The king's son, Sextus, raped a noblewoman named Lucretia. With no prospect of justice, this proved the final straw. The nobles rose up, led by Lucius Junius Brutus, making the name prominent in the Roman mind (and of course a similarly named man was involved in Julius Caesar's assassination over four centuries later). Tarquinius was overthrown and the republic established. One of Brutus's first acts was to swear an oath that Rome would never again be ruled by a king. In this mythology was born the Roman aversion to kingship, so strong that even emperors avoided using the word, even though they held the same power.

Interestingly, archaeological evidence suggests the presence of a small village as far back as 1000 BC.[3] An inscription referring to 'RECEI', an early Latin form of *rex* was found under the forum in Rome in AD 1899, leading some to believe there may be elements of truth in the tales.[4] Let us

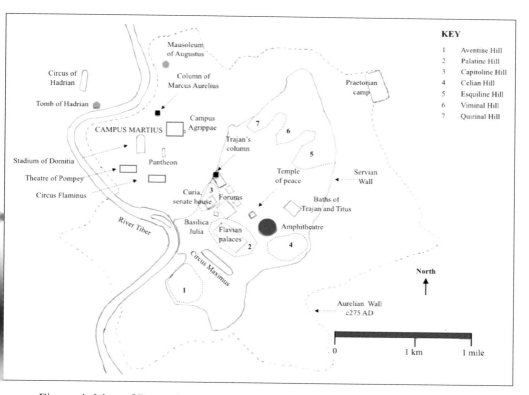

Figure 4: Map of Rome 1st to 3rd centuries AD.

now turn to the republican period and how Rome developed upon to the Principate. We will leave this section with a map of Rome in the first to third centuries. It is worth noting the position of the Flavian Palaces and Flavian Amphitheatre which we know today as the Colosseum.

The Republic

The republican system allegedly born out of Brutus's civil war involved the election of two consuls, voted for by the people. These held office for a year and presided over the election of their successors. This balance of power between two consuls and a group of senators was to last for hundreds of years but could not survive the rapid expansion that led to the establishment of Imperial rule. It could be said that the most successful emperors were those who maintained the illusion that they were merely first among equals and treated the senate with respect, such as Antonius Pius and Marcus Aurelius. Those who treated them with disdain, such as Caligula and Commodus, tended to meet rather stickier ends.

During the early republic, one man exemplified the concept of the ideal leader that many later emperors would try to live up to, or at least claim to. Around 458 BC the Aequi, a tribe to the east of Rome, broke their treaty and destroyed a Roman army sent out to deal with them. A second army became besieged. Panicking senators appointed Lucius Quinctius Cincinnatus as dictator to deal with the emergency. The word 'dictator' does not have the same connotations as it does today. Here it was an official post, with specific powers for a set time, appointed to deal with an emergency. Cincinnatus duly defeated the Aequi, disbanded his army and stepped down, just fifteen days after his appointment. Twenty years later he served as dictator again, this time for just twenty-one days.

The Romans revered him for his service and selfless patriotism. He became the ideal of virtue and civic duty. In the eighteenth century The Society of Cincinnati was formed in the United States and France and Cincinnatus gave his name to the city in Ohio. Some emperors certainly ignored these fine ideals but others at least paid lip service to this reluctance to retain and abuse power. The ideal of the republican system, if not the reality, can be seen in the phrase 'Senatus Populusque Romanus', 'the Senate and People of Rome', SPQR. Interestingly, when trying to raise money for his extravagant games, Commodus reversed the word order, 'Populus Senatusque', putting the people before the senate. This might play well to modern ears but, to many second-century Romans, this was dangerous populism. To the senatorial class, it was another cause of deep resentment.

Political and social upheaval during the 'conflict of orders' (c. BC 500–287) resulted in the Plebian Council and the 'Laws of the Twelve Tables', displayed in the forum. This laid out the rights and duties of all Roman citizens, resulting in a further balance and separation of powers. The Roman Republic flourished and expanded throughout the Italian peninsula and began to spread across the Mediterranean. It was perhaps inevitable it would come into conflict with that other great power of the ancient world, Carthage. Three wars were fought between 264-146 BC, the second of which involved the famous Hannibal, who nearly brought Rome to its knees. But it was Rome that emerged victorious and Carthage that was destroyed.

The exact date for the change to empire is debatable. Some point to Caesar's crossing of the Rubicon in 49. Others date it to his defeat of Pompey the Great at Pharsalus in the following year, after his appointment as consul. Two years later he was appointed dictator for ten years. There would be no handing back of power this time as with Cincinnatus. Yet Caesar was never declared *imperator*.

However, perhaps the seeds of these events were sown not during a time of conflict but a decade before. In 60 BC three powerful men formed a pact. Pompey, Crassus and Julius Caesar took control behind the scenes and dominated the appointment of consuls, military commands and key decisions.[5] Crassus would die with his legions at Carrhae in 53 BC, Pompeii after his defeat to Caesar.

In 44 BC Caesar's assassins were to invoke the memory of the overthrow of Tarquinius by Brutus, centuries before. Among their chief complaints was that Caesar was a tyrant who wished to be a king, something many Romans could not stomach. Another Brutus claimed to be a saviour of the Roman Republic. But this time was different. Civil war ensued and Brutus and many of his co-conspirators were to fall at the Battle of Philippi. The Second Triumvirate of Octavian, Mark Antony and Lepidus lasted little more than a decade. The subsequent civil war and defeat of Mark Antony left Octavian the sole ruler of the Roman world.

Some no doubt considered this ancient history by the time of Vespasian's birth. The climactic battle of Actium was four decades in the past. Augustus had been officially emperor for 36 years. Republican sentiment may have lingered among some but there was to be no going back. Before looking at the imperial period it would be useful to note the social and political structures at the time.

Social structure

The Roman social structure was deeply hierarchical with clear boundaries and class distinctions. In early republican times the divide was between the ruling patricians and the plebeians, the latter of which formed the bulk of the population. In republican times a small number of old families, often wealthy landowners, jostled for supremacy. The early emperors would emerge from one of those very families. During the republic a distinction emerged between the senatorial class, from the old patrician families, and what became the equestrian class. This second group provided the majority of the financial administrators and junior military officers. The provincial governors and legionary commanders were drawn from the senatorial class.

Beneath this ruling elite came the bulk of the population. By the first century the plebeians were a formal class who held their own elections. They consisted of all free Roman citizens who were not members of the senatorial or equestrian classes. These included farmers, builders and craftsmen. In the early principate, only Roman citizens could join the legions and this provided one of the few routes for promotion. For example, an able soldier could be promoted through the ranks to *primus pilus* ('first spear'), the leading centurion of a legion, which gave him access to the equestrian class.

Auxiliary units were made up of barbarian troops, non-Roman citizens. The granting of citizenship after twenty-five years of service was a major attraction. Vespasian was to relax the rules and allow Roman citizens into the auxiliaries. In addition, the auxiliary unit commanders were Roman equestrians. These included barbarian leaders who had been granted Roman citizenship. This distinction between the legions and auxiliaries lasted until the reign of Caracalla in the early third century.

Below the plebeians came freedmen, former slaves, who had been granted manumission by a magistrate. This gave them Roman citizenship, but they were not allowed to hold office. Their sons were, and one famous example saw such a son of a freedman rise to equestrian status through a successful military career. He would eventually be promoted to the senatorial class and ultimately gain the throne. That man was Pertinax in 193, a remarkable feat for the son of a freedman. However, it indicates that, despite the apparent rigidity of the social hierarchy, social advancement was possible.

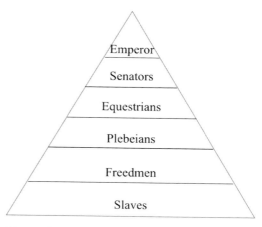

Figure 5: Social order in first century Rome.

What is important to note is that emperors such as Marcus Aurelius were careful to respect tradition and, crucially, the senate. Men such as Pompieanus, Maximianus and Pertinax were all from the equestrian class, but Marcus maintained the distinction, promoting them into the senate before they were given roles as legion commanders or governors. Many of the problems Commodus experienced with the senate came about because he disrespected them and promoted freedmen to positions of authority over senators.

At the bottom of society came the slaves. Owners could beat, brand or even kill their slaves. By the second century, one fifth of the world's population lived under Roman rule, and about 10 to 15 per cent, 7-10 million, were slaves. Most of the population, around 80 per cent, lived in rural areas, leaving 20 per cent in towns and cities, 400 of which dotted the Italian peninsula alone. In Rome it has been estimated that up to half of the one million population were slaves.

Senatorial and equestrian careers

High levels of inequality existed with access to the higher echelons of society based on property qualifications. To become a senator required one million sesterces whilst equestrian rank was set at 400,000 sesterces. In the first century, Augustus reduced the number of senators from 900 to 600, from which he appointed governors of provinces and legates, commanders of legions. Equestrians numbered approximately 30,000 with around 2,000 in Rome. From this group were appointed tribunes or procurators to assist governors. They also provided the bulk of junior officers, acting as commanders of auxiliary units and legionary military tribunes, advising the senatorial legates. Prefects of the Praetorian Guard in Rome, one of the four great prefectures, were always equestrians.

To serve as a juror required 200,000 sesterces, whilst Municipal councillors required approximately 100,000 sesterces. The bulk of Roman citizens were either salaried workers (doctors, teachers, municipal workers and shop owners) or those working a hand-to-mouth existence. To put this into perspective, a peasant family needed 500 sesterces a year. Average wages were just four sesterces a day (less than 1,500 a year), slightly more than the 1,200 a legionary received. Equestrian procurators (financial administrators) earned between 60,000 to 300,000 sesterces whereas a senatorial governor received 400,000. Cicero reportedly earned 555,555 sesterces for his legal work alone.[6] A moderately wealthy man had an income 714 times greater than a pauper, while for the very rich it was over 10,000 times.

Inequality was built into the very fabric of society. Patronage was also an important concept. An individual from a lower order could receive help in the form of money, food or legal aid. Most importantly, it opened doors to advancement. A powerful *patronus* might facilitate a plebeian's access to equestrian status. A position on the *tres militiae*, the career path of the equestrian class, beckoned. This can be seen in figure 6.

This began with command of an auxiliary infantry unit. In the reign of Claudius the next step was command of a cavalry regiment before becoming military tribune of a legion, *tribunus angusticlavius*. After Nero, the last two posts switched with many tribunes going on to command a cavalry *ala*. Thus, by the time of Vespasian a cavalry commander was the senior post.

Those showing promise or demonstrating loyalty might obtain a position as a procurator. This was a type of financial officer who reported directly to the emperor. Each province had its own equestrian procurator although the provincial governor tended to be of senatorial rank, with some exceptions. Minor provinces, temporary commands and the strategically important example of Egypt were administered by only the most trusted equestrians. Finally came one of the four great praefectures:

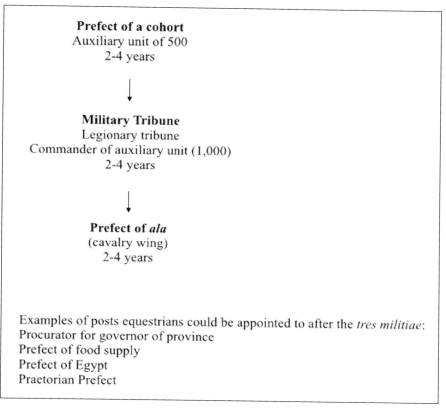

Prefect of a cohort
Auxiliary unit of 500
2-4 years

Military Tribune
Legionary tribune
Commander of auxiliary unit (1,000)
2-4 years

Prefect of *ala*
(cavalry wing)
2-4 years

Examples of posts equestrians could be appointed to after the *tres militiae*:
Procurator for governor of province
Prefect of food supply
Prefect of Egypt
Praetorian Prefect

Figure 6: The equestrian military career path, *Tres militia.*

- Prefect of the grain supply, *praefectus annonae*, again based in Rome.
- Prefect of the Vigiles, *praefectus vigilum*, commanding seven cohorts, also in Rome.
- Prefect of Egypt, *praefectus Aegypti*, controlling the strategically important province of Egypt with its number of legions and importance of its grain supply.
- Praetorian prefect, *praefectus praetorius*, based in Rome and consisting of usually nine cohorts.

During the first century AD, emperors began to award *equis publicus* without the need of the censor. By the second century it had become common to be a gift of the emperor. There are many examples of equestrians being promoted to the senate after an illustrious military career or one of the four great *praefectures*. In later centuries the position of Praetorian Prefect was to be pivotal in many a palace intrigue resulting in the death of more than one emperor.

The senatorial career would often begin in the early twenties as a military tribune in a legion. Here he would be second in command to a senatorial legionary legate but advised by five equestrian military tribunes in the middle of the *tres militiae*. These were often battle-hardened experienced soldiers, some rising through the ranks to obtain equestrian status via the *primus pilus*, 'first spear', the senior centurion of the legion.

The career path for a young man of senatorial status was the *cursus honorum*, 'course of honour' or, more commonly, 'ladder of offices'. This gave aspiring nobles a route to high office. The first step on this ladder as a military tribune, *tribunus laticlavius*, was followed by different magistracies: quaestor; aedile; praetor; consul. These all had different roles and minimum ages which were often disregarded for politically important appointments.

The next chapter will detail Vespasian's early career until he was appointed legate and found himself heading towards the coast of Britain in AD 43. Governors and legionary commanders were chosen from praetors and consuls, hence terms such as propraetorian or proconsul governor. In addition to the requirement to have one million sesterces, senatorial status was hereditary for three generations with no obligation of taking office.

Becoming consul or governing a province was considered a plum job. Vast sums of money could be earned from administering a region rich in resources as well as power and influence from the networks of patronage. It is important at this point to note how the provincial system functioned in the first century and during Vespasian's reign in particular.

Two main types of provinces existed: Senatorial and Imperial. Senatorial provinces were under the command of a governor of senatorial rank who reported to the senate, in theory at least. With the exception of minor provinces and Egypt, Imperial provinces were administered by those of senatorial rank who reported directly to the emperor. These men were ex-consuls or praetors, hence the titles *proconsul* or *propraetorian* legate. Legionary commanders were also appointed by the emperor. Provinces with a single legion were administered by the same man, the pro-praetorian legate of the emperor, often seen on inscriptions as *legatus Augusti pro praetore*.

As the empire developed, more provinces came under control of the emperor and the senate had less and less power. The subsequent reign of Augustus, 27 BC to AD 14, saw a number of reforms. Senatorial decrees were

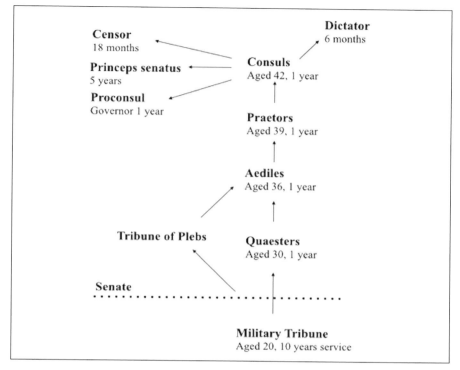

Figure 7: The Cursus Honorum.

given the force of law along with Imperial pronouncements which together formed the basis of Roman legislation. Senators became an arm of the state and subordinate to the emperor. By the time of Vespasian, the emperor had control of the appointments of all legionary legates, senatorial tribunes and most provincial governors. In addition, all procurators reported directly to him, leaving the senate with a handful of minor provinces to rubber-stamp imperial decrees. We can see how the structure of government changed between the republic and the empire in figures 8 and 9.

The last figure shows the extent of the Roman Empire at the time of Vespasian's birth. Rome then spread from the deserts of Arabia in the east to the forests or shores of the great ocean in the west, beyond which lay the mysterious island where Vespasian would forge his reputation. Egypt was firmly under Roman control and provided important grain imports for the citizens of Rome. But the Romans could not be complacent. To the east the Parthians were a constant threat. But the year Vespasian was born also marked one of the greatest defeats in Roman history.

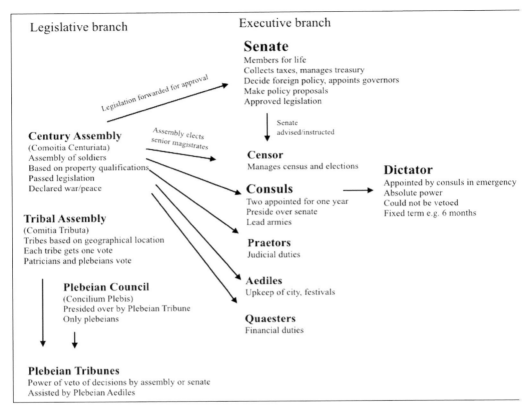

Figure 8: Governmental structure under the Roman Republic.

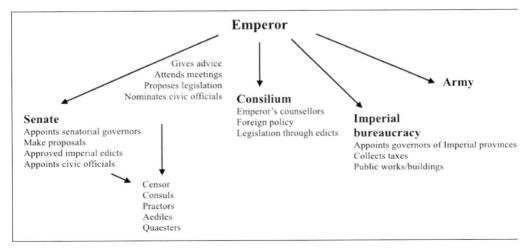

Figure 9: Governmental structure under the Roman Empire.

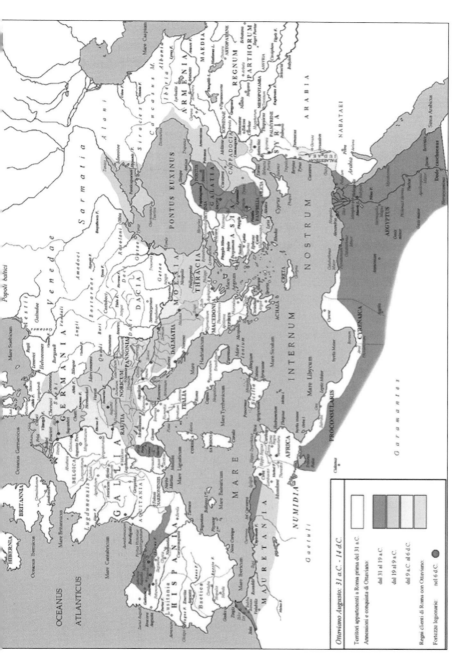

Figure 10: The Roman Empire at the time of Augustus Caesar. (Wikimedia Commons)

Chapter 2

VESPASIAN'S EARLY LIFE

Titus Flavius Vespasianus came into the world on the evening of 17 November AD 9, the year that the Romans suffered a devastating defeat in the Teutoburg Forest in Germania. It was there that the Roman general Varus led three legions to destruction against Germanic tribesmen. A disaster that caused the first emperor, Augustus, to literally bang his head against the walls of his palace in anguish yelling, *Quintili Vare, legiones redde*, 'Quintilius Varus, give me back my legions'.

Vespasian was born in a hamlet in the beautiful Sabine country a short distance to the north-east of Rome. He had two siblings, an elder brother, Sabinus, and an unnamed sister who died in infancy. The goal for any ambitious equestrian family was to see their sons rise to a magistracy and possibly even the senate. Sabinus would grow to be the first of the Flavii to achieve this senatorial rank. However, there was nothing to suggest the greatness that lay ahead for this equestrian family.

Vespasian's paternal grandfather, T. Flavius Petro of Reate, was a centurion in the civil war between Julius Caesar and Pompey. Unfortunately for the family's prospects, he had fought on the losing side at Pharsalus in 48 BC. Caesar, often magnanimous, granted pardons and honourable discharges for many such men and Flavius found himself a role in civilian life as a debt collector. He married a woman from Etruria, Tertulla, and they had a son, Vespasian's father, Flavius Sabinus.

The career of Vespasian's father is not certain, with some suggesting a military career up to *primus pilus*, the lead centurion in a legion. This would have automatically made him eligible for equestrian status on retirement. However, Suetonius claims he was a banker, or money-lender, and did no military service. Later detractors of Vespasian would point to a poor childhood where he was reduced to manual labour on his parents' farm. Sabinus senior served during the reigns of Augustus and Tiberius, probably in Gaul. Luckily for Vespasian his father married up.

Vespasia Polla came from an aspiring family. Her father had served as *praefectus castrorum*, camp prefect, and *tribunus*, military tribune, three times, indicating that he was a *tribunus angusticlavius*. Both ranks signified his equestrian status. Her brother had been promoted to the senate, obtaining a praetorship. Vespasia was ambitious and had similar hopes for her sons.

Vespasian was brought up by his paternal grandmother, Tertulla, at Cosa in Ertruria. The land was mountainous and forested to the north but to the south were olive groves, vineyards and good farmland which supported livestock and crops. It was to remain a favourite spot for Vespasian, and he would return throughout his life to enjoy the warm summers and beautiful scenery. Indeed, he died at Cutiliae near Cittaducale very close to where he was born.

The death of the first emperor in the year 14 saw the ascension of Tiberius whom the senate confirmed as *princeps*, a term originating in the republican era meaning 'first in time or order'. It is from this word we get the word *principate* to describe the period between the republic and the reign of Diocletian in the late third century (from whom the period dominate is derived after the title *dominatus*, 'lord' or 'master').

More thrilling for the now 5-year-old Vespasian would have been news from Germania. There the general Germanicus Julius Caesar was avenging Rome's greatest defeat, cutting a swathe through Germanic tribes and hunting down Arminius, chieftain of the Cherusci and commander of the Germanic troops at Teutoburg. Germanicus was adopted by Tiberius and became a favourite among the soldiers and people. His early death in the year 19 was suspicious and showed just how brutal and deadly Roman politics could be. Among the children of Germanicus was the 7-year-old Gaius Caesar Augustus Germanicus, better known to history as Caligula. Germanicus had a brother, and uncle to Caligula, Claudius. Both men were to have a pivotal effect on Vespasian's career.

Details of Vespasian's childhood are unknown but he would have received the *toga virilis*, toga of manhood, at around age 16, c. 25-6. His older brother applied to wear the *latus clavus* (tunic with a broad stripe), worn by members of the senatorial order. Sabinus having achieved senatorial status, the pressure was on the younger brother to emulate him. Suetonius claims Vespasian was reluctant, but his mother urged him to follow in his brother's footsteps, chiding him as his brother's 'footman' and 'dependent'. It seems he eventually relented and held a military post soon after, perhaps serving in Thrace with one of the Moesian legions. Vespasian was set on a pathway his mother hoped would lead to senatorial status like his brother. Let us first take a brief look at the equestrian order into which he was born.

Equestrians

The equestrian order had its origins in the mounted aristocracy of the pre-republican period. At the time of the last king, Tarquinus, it is estimated that there were 1,800 cavalrymen. During the early republic, c. 400 BC, any male citizen was allowed to serve as an *eques*. However, the condition was that he had to bring his own horse. It became not an economic class, but an 'occupational status group'.[1] As the republic grew, the wealthiest became the landowning elite and those elites were allowed to be *equites*, serving for ten years.

A distinction developed. Rich landowners and members of the most powerful families were provided horses by the state and termed *equites equo publico*. Out of this elite group, 300, often the wealthiest, formed the senate. Citizens from the general population who met the property requirements were known as equites, *equo publico suo*, literally 'cavalry on their own horse'. The latter outnumbered the former by 23,000 to 1,800.[2] Censors had to legitimise property qualifications to formally promote someone into the order. The distinction between the senatorial class and a separate equestrian order was to come much later.

In the late second century BC, aspiring senators had formally to give up their horses and two separate orders evolved out of the early *equites*: *ordo senatorius* and *ordo equester*. A law of 129 BC removed senators from the class of equites altogether. By around 100 BC we get the first reference of an *ordo equester*. Both orders were above the general population, the *plebeians*, who, in turn, had more rights as citizens than freedmen and slaves.

Occasionally EQUES, or EQ, is found on honorific or finery monuments, the earliest example being in c. 100 BC.[3] However, the usual practice was to record civilian or military posts although sometimes the phrase *honoris et virtutis causa* appears, referring to the equestrian virtues of honour and valour.

Pliny the Elder credits Cicero for legitimising the equestrian order, promoting it within the *res publica*, the Roman legal system, protected by *concordia ordinum*, 'harmony of the orders'. The enfranchisement of Roman citizenship had been extending to other Italian cities and, by the time of Augustus, Italian *eques* who had never set foot in Rome could be classed as equestrians. Roman institutions had moved beyond the confines of the once city state.

As time moved on the more prestigious roles were given to senatorial families. They could be elected as magistrates, command legions and were banned from direct involvement with trade and commerce. To distinguish themselves, certain symbols developed: a broad stripe on their tunic, *latus clavus*; a gold ring, *anulus aureus*; and privileges such as the front row at the theatre.

As the republic expanded and new territories were conquered, auxiliary troops became more important as did a multitude of civilian roles. It was necessary to find adequate numbers of loyal, educated and capable men to command auxiliary units and serve as legionary military tribunes. Rome also needed financial administrators, tax collectors, jurors and junior magistrates. The equestrians seemed the natural choice. These *Equites Romani* also acquired status symbols such as gold rings, tunics with a narrow stripe, *angustus clavus*, specific ceremonies and certain privileges, such as the front fourteen rows at theatres.

By the time of Vespasian the career path was well entrenched. The pinnacle of such a career might be a procurator of a province or even an equestrian governor of a minor province such as Sardinia. For a select few, one of the four great prefectures of Rome awaited or possibly even promotion to the senate. Equestrian numbers rose from 15,000 during the republic to 20,000–30,000 under the empire and remained the main source of new entries to the senate, which fluctuated between 300 and 600.

Despite the rigidity of the social system, we have seen that examples of social advancement did exist. As well as Pertinax, emperor briefly in 193, the poet Horace was the son of a freed slave. Augustus introduced various reforms for the equestrian order: setting social and moral standards, creating priesthoods and increasing their numbers and positions. Many were directly appointed provincial governors and financial administrators, acts intended to make them more dependent on, and loyal to, the emperor.

In the first century there were thirty procurator posts, but by the mid-third century this had risen to 180.[4] In each generation only 600 out of the 30,000 equestrians rose to hold the post of procurator. This group, about 2 per cent, became an elite group within the order, referred to by Tacitus as *equestris nobilitis* – equestrian nobility. In later centuries equestrians became more a civilian, as opposed to a military, elite. Further classes appeared: *Egregius* and *perfectissimus* at the top, and *eques Romanus* at the bottom. Property qualifications became less significant, and officers were promoted directly into positions and given equestrian status automatically.

During the Crisis of the Third Century, under Gallienus (c 260-268), senators lost the right to command legions to equestrians. Successive emperors trusted senators less and less and power shifted to the military. From the late third century, more emperors emerged from this route than the traditional senatorial career path. All that was in the future and in Vespasian's time the equestrians had a clearly defined role, career path and route to the higher social status of the senate.

During the reign of Augustus, cavalry commands had become exclusively equestrian and, under subsequent emperors, duties expanded to tax collecting and judicial roles. Posts titled *praefectus* also appeared within provinces covering tribal areas or part of a frontier with a senatorial legate in overall command. Emperors began to award *equis publicus* without the need of the censor and by the time of Marcus Aurelius it had become common to be a gift of the emperor.

Claudius had expanded on the reforms of Augustus and imposed a fixed hierarchy on the *tres militiae*: prefect of cohort; prefect of cavalry; legionary military tribune. Nero switched the last two posts making a *praefectus alae* the senior post. Vespasian served in a military post in Thrace c. 25-27 under Tiberius although in what capacity is unknown. By his early twenties he appears to have gained a foot on the next rung of the social ladder. His mother would no doubt have beamed with pride and satisfaction. Both her sons were now of senatorial rank.

The Road to Britannia

The quaestorship was the first magistracy that allowed access to the senate. To achieve this, Vespasian is thought to have served two periods of service, one in the military and one in a minor magistracy. He may have finished the first in Thrace by c. 30, under Tiberius, before obtaining a position in the *Vigintivirate*. This placed him in charge of street-cleaning and executions. At the age of about 24 in c. 33-4, he was appointed a quaestor in the province of Crete with Cyrene. The post was not particularly prestigious, but it opened up the next opportunity. He managed to obtain the next step on the *cursus honorum*, as an *aedile*, on his second attempt, elected in last place and holding office in 38. Tiberius had died the year before and was succeeded by the 25-year-old Caligula.

Vespasian had an inauspicious start to his senatorial career. As *aedile* one of his responsibilities was keeping the streets clean. The new emperor noticed a particularly dirty alley and ordered dirt to be thrown at Vespasian's toga as punishment. This doesn't seem to have held up his career as he received a praetorship in 39-40. One possible explanation may have been his long-standing relationship with Antonia Caenis, a freedwoman and confidante of the emperor's grandmother, Antonia. The latter died shortly after her grandson's accession, but her contacts gave Vespasian access to a network of influential people. Caenis would prove to be a major influence in Vespasian's life.

Caligula's reign was to last less than four years. Contemporary writers and later historians paint a picture of an arrogant, petty and murderous young man. Others declare him insane, citing his wish to make his horse a senator and his growing belief in his own divinity. His disrespect of the senate and equestrian order lost him support. He was eventually stabbed to death in an underground passage beneath the palace on the Palatine Hill. The deed was performed by the commander of the Praetorian Guard, Chaerea, disgruntled at being the butt of Caligula's mocking.

Whilst Chaerea had support from various senators and equestrians, his men were not universally behind him. Caligula's Germanic guard went on a killing spree to avenge their fallen emperor. Innocent bystanders were caught up as well as some of the murderers and co-conspirators: Caligula's wife, Caesonia, was stabbed by a centurion, while his daughter's brains were dashed out against a wall. As the praetorians sacked, looted and murdered anyone they came across, a single guardsman wandered through the palace. A curtain twitched and caught his eye. He saw toes poking out from beneath the drapes and drew them back. There he found Caligula's uncle, Claudius, shaking with fear.

The 51-year-old Claudius fell at his feet in terror and the fate of the empire hung in the balance. A different guardsman may have sent history in an altogether different direction. However, this praetorian hailed the quaking figure 'emperor'. Claudius was dragged to the praetorians and again fate intervened. Rather than being hacked down with the others he was placed on a litter and carried back to their camp. A reluctant Claudius sent a message back to the senate claiming he was held against his will. The senate descended into bickering whilst Suetonius claims the people called for Claudius and thus, with the power of the mob and thousands of vengeful bloodthirsty praetorians breathing down their necks, the senate accepted the inevitable. The most unlikely of emperors now sat on the throne, old, sickly and reluctant. But it was under Claudius that Vespasian was to find glory. In Britannia.

It was likely during Caligula's reign that Vespasian married Flavia Domitilla. Their first son Titus was born in late 39. A second son, and another future emperor, Domitian, arrived over a decade later. It must have been a difficult task, climbing the greasy political pole whilst avoiding Caligula's whims. Roman writers portray him as a murderous psychopath who once threw an entire section of the audience into the arena to be killed by the beasts because he was bored.[5] Vespasian could easily have ended up as one of Caligula's victims.

However, the emperor's assassination, and Claudius's ascension, opened the door to a bright future. Early in his reign he appointed Vespasian legate of *Legio II Augusta*. Vespasian's first legionary command was in Germany, guarding the same Rhine frontier where Varus lost three legions decades before in the year of Vespasian's birth. As a boy he had grown up hearing of the exploits and victories of Germanicus, long dead brother of Emperor Claudius. He may also have heard that the Second Augusta played a significant role. Now a man, he found himself leading one of the legions Germanicus led to victory. Guarding the same border, looking out at the same dark, dense forests Germanicus had cut a swathe through a generation before.

Legio II Augusta

Legion II Augusta was stationed at Argentoratum, Strasbourg, in Germania Superior. Vespasian owed his appointment partly to Narcissus, Claudius's most powerful freedman. As we shall see, it was this same

Narcissus who encouraged the reluctant legionaries to board ship two years later in the invasion of Britannia. Figure 11 portrays the Rhine frontier in the first year of Vespasian's reign. Back in the early 40s Britain was yet to be conquered but the base at Argentoratum can be seen towards the bottom of the map.

Vespasian seems to have seen action since Josephus later claimed he restored peace to the west after unrest in Germania. The legion is thought to have been formed by Julius Caesar in 48 BC or possibly by Octavian just after Caesar's assassination. Their emblems included Capricorn, the winged horse Pegasus and the war god Mars although by the late third century only the first had survived. It is thought to have originally been called *Sabina* meaning 'from the Sabine country', which would have appealed to Vespasian, given his upbringing.

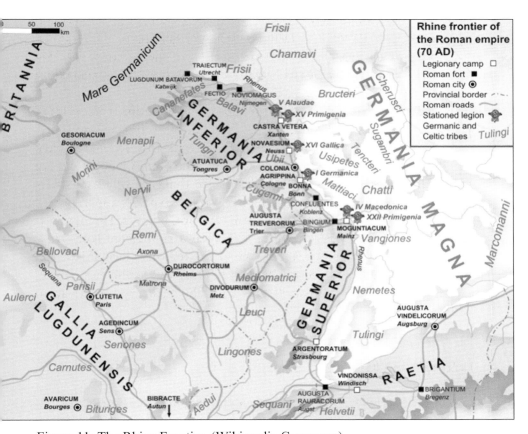

Figure 11: The Rhine Frontier. (Wikimedia Commons)

The Second fought at Philippi in 42 BC under the Second Triumvirate when Octavian, Mark Antony and Lepidus defeated Brutus and his co-conspirators. Slingshots bearing the mark *Caesar Leg II* suggest it was present at the siege of Perugia the following year. By 30 BC it was in Hispania Tarraconensis fighting in the Cantabrian War of 26-19 BC. After the disaster in the Teutoburg Forest in AD 9 it was moved to the Rhine where it fought under Germanicus in 14-16. Sometime later it moved to a new base at Agentoratum protecting a major crossing point of the Rhine and was noted for a victory against Gallic rebels c. AD 21.

As we shall see in the next chapter it was one of the four legions that was to invade Britain in 43. First based at Silchester, it later moved to Dorchester, Dorset. By the year 55 it had moved farther west to Exeter where it remained for nearly two decades. After a short time at Gloucester, it finally arrived at what was to be its home for three centuries, Caerleon in South Wales.

Legionary units would often form *vexillations* and be sent to plug gaps elsewhere. One such vexillation of the Second supported Vitellius in the 'Year of the Four Emperors' in 69 when he marched on Rome, prompting Otho's suicide (Galba, the first of the four contenders having already been killed by the praetorian guard months before). Vespasian's subsequent victory sent those units back to Britain where the bulk of the Second remained.

The Second played a role in Agricola's great victory at Mons Graupius in 83. Substantial evidence shows them engaged in road building and the construction of both Hadrian's and the Antonine walls. In 196 Clodius Albinus took much of the garrison from Britain to Gaul, only to be defeated at Lugdunum the following year. The victor of that battle, Septimius Severus, used the legion in his Caledonian campaign of 208-11. The Second shared a large fortress at Carpow on the River Tay with the Sixth Legion from York. Later it received the name *Antonina*, implying its loyalty to either Caracalla or Elagabalus.

Its main base remained Caerleon into the mid-third century. Reforms under Diocletian and Constantine I split legions into smaller units. The last known reference for the Second is found in an early-fifth-century document, *Notitia Dignatatum*. This lists a unit under the command of the *Comes Litoris Soxonicum per Britannias*, 'Count of the Saxon Shore': *Praefectus legionis secundae Augustae, Rutupis* (Commander of the Second Legion Augusta, Richborough, Kent). The legion may have been withdrawn to Gaul and disappeared in the upheavals of the fifth century.

Under Vespasian in the first century the legion would have had a paper strength of 5,120 heavy infantry, command staff, 120 legionary cavalry and a variety of people essential to maintaining a camp: engineers, craftsmen, vets, surgeons and many others. He had inherited a battle-hardened fighting force. The next section will detail the structure of a typical legion.

The legion

Under Augustus Caesar there were approximately twenty-five legions, a number that was to rise steadily to thirty-five by the time of Caracalla in the early third century. In the first century a legion numbered approximately 5,500 and consisted of professional volunteers drawn from Roman citizens. Vespasian, as the legion commander, was titled *legatus* legionis. Such men were always of senatorial rank and served for an average of three to four years.

In provinces with more than one legion the legate would answer to the provincial governor, the *legatus Augusti pro praetore*. Where there was only one legion present in a province the *legatus legionis* was also the governor. In the invasion of 43 alongside Vespasian as *legatus legionis* of *Legio II Augusta* were three other legionary commanders. One was named Gnaeus Hosidius Geta although it is not known which legion he led. Both men reported to Aulus Plautius, the general in charge of the invasion force. He was to become the first governor of the new province, *Britannia*.

Back with the Second Augusta the second in command was a senatorial tribune, *tribunus laticlavius*, 'military tribune of the broad stripe', often an inexperienced young man, perhaps the son of a senator, gaining some military experience before starting on the *cursus honorum*. His next experience of military matters might well be as legate himself should he reach a praetorship or even consul. Vespasian's son Titus was to serve as a *tribunus laticlavius* in Britain after Boudicca's revolt of c. 60-1, although it is not known in which legion he served.

Alongside our young senatorial tribune were five equestrian tribunes, *tribuni angusticlavii*, 'military tribune of the narrow stripe'. These were often experienced, battle-hardened men. At the time of the invasion this formed the last rung on the ladder of promotion for equestrians, the *tres militiae*. Such a man would already have served as a *praefectus cohortis* and *praefectus alae*. Both posts placed them in charge of auxiliary units where they often formed the first line of battle. At Mons Graupius it was the Germanic auxiliary units who attacked first, led by their Roman equestrian officers.

The third in command was the *praefectus castrorum*, camp prefect. An experienced career soldier in his fifties, he may well have risen through the ranks to achieve *primus pilus*. He was in charge of the camp, training, maintenance and logistics but would take command when the legate and his second in command were absent. Thus the senior officers of a legion consisted of the following:

> First in command: Senatorial legionary commander, *legatus legionis*.
>
> Second in command: Senatorial tribune, *tribunus laticlavius*.
>
> Advisors: Five equestrian military tribunes, *tribuni angusticlavii*.
>
> Third in command: Camp prefect, *praefectus castrorum*.

The legate and his command staff were joined in the command tent by the *primus pilus*, the lead centurion of the legion. The legion itself was made up of ten cohorts with cohorts 2 to 10 divided into six centuries, each of eighty men, thus 480 per cohort. The lead centurion of each was called the *pilus prior*. The first cohort, however, consisted of five double centuries of 160 men, totalling 800 men. The lead centurion of this elite cohort was the *primus pilus*, who led the first century, *centuria*, of the first cohort. He obtained equestrian class on retirement.

Therefore, there were fifty-nine centurions in a legion, each with an *optio* as second in command. Each century was made up of ten (or twenty in the first cohort) eight-man 'tent groups', *contubernium*, who shared a mess tent and a mule.[6] Each century had a *signifier* who carried the standard for the century. He was also responsible for the troop's pay and savings. Accompanying him was a *cornicen* or horn blower, and an *imaginifer*, carrying an image of the emperor to remind the men of their loyalty. One last point concerns battle standards. The *aquilifer* carried the legion's standard or eagle. The legions used three main types of military signals: the 'voiced'; the 'semi-voiced', with bugle, horn or trumpet;

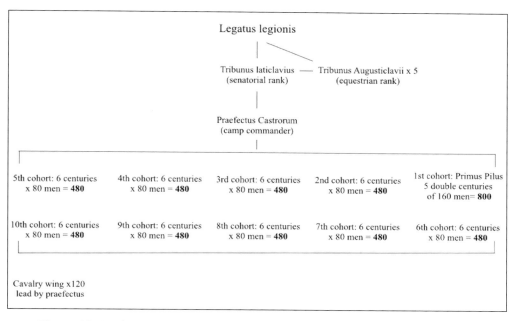

Figure 12: Legion structure in the first century AD.

and the 'mute signals', with eagles, dragons, ensigns and plumes.[7] While the eagle was the standard of the Roman legions, later cohorts had their own 'dragon-bearer'.[8] In addition to the 5,120 infantry, the legion had a 120-man *alae*, cavalry, attached called the *eques legionis*, used as scouts and messengers.

Vespasian's command staff would thus have included his second in command, a young senatorial tribune, *tribunus laticlavius*, five equestrian tribunes, *tribunus Augusticlavii*, the camp commander, *praefectus castrorum* and the senior centurion, *primus pilus*. Often auxiliary units would be attached for a specific campaign. Normally the equestrian commanders would answer to the provincial governor in whose province they served rather than the nearest legionary base. Attached to Vespasian's legion on campaign they answered to him.

Auxiliaries

Prior to Claudius, auxiliary commands were given to senators, equestrians or *primipilares* on an ad hoc fashion. By the year 43 both the organisation of auxiliary units and career path of equestrians became more organised. Auxiliary units had often been temporary and named after the commander or tribe. Now they were permanent and their original ethnic names, such as Cohors I Tungrorum, were no longer an indication of the ethnic makeup of the unit.

In battle the legions provided the heavy infantry and it was the auxiliaries who provided the bulk of the light troops and cavalry. During the invasion of 43, at both the Medway and Thames, Germanic auxiliaries were deployed first. As at Mons Graupius, if the enemy broke, the cavalry and light troops could pursue. If this failed, the enemy could be lured onto the legions. Here stood an impenetrable wall of wood and iron and if an initial wild charge did not break the formation the attackers would often be doomed, forced backwards over their dead and injured by an advancing wall of deadly swords.

Auxiliary troops became more important during the principate, numbering as many as 440 units by the mid-second century, half of which were stationed in the Danube provinces.[9] There were three main types of these units: infantry; cavalry; and mixed. Each could be a standard unit of around 500, *quingeneria*, or a larger unit termed a *milliaria*. This latter one was not always literally one thousand but varied in size as we can see in the table below.

Table 1: Auxiliary unit types

Unit	Description	Number	Composition
Cohors quingeneria peditata	Infantry	480	6 centuries of 80
Ala quingenaria	Cavalry	480	16 turmae of 30
Cohors equitata quingeneria	Mixed	600	480 infantry, 120 cavalry
Cohors milliaria peditata	Infantry	800	10 centuries of 80
Ala milliaria	Cavalry	720	24 turmae of 32
Cohors equitata milliaria	Mixed	1040	800 infantry, 240 cavalry

In the early principate a *primus pilus* could move on to command an auxiliary unit. However, by the second century nearly all auxiliary commanders came from the established equestrian class, often beginning their careers as magistrates in Italian and, later provincial, municipal cities.[10] Most unit commanders were termed *praefectus*, although some were of tribune rank.

Claudian reforms standardised the career path for equestrians so that at the time of the invasion an aspiring equestrian might serve as a *praefectus cohortis*, then command a cavalry unit, *praefectus alae*, finishing as a military tribune of a legion, *tribunus militum*. The period of service for a commander was not fixed but was usually two to four years.

Claudius began granting bronze diplomas giving auxiliaries Roman citizenship after 25 years' service. This grant was extended to their wives and children. Two other kinds of units are worth mentioning.[11] First, *numeri* was a term used for a body of irregular troops. One example was of a unit of Britons posted to the German frontier manning a series of watchtowers. Another example is a *numerus* of bargemen from the Tigris at South Shields on the Tyne in northern Britain. Second, *cunei* appears to be specifically a Germanic irregular unit. Literally meaning 'wedge', Tacitus refers to this Germanic tactic of attack, and applies it to the Batavii in the civil war of 69.

Vespasian would work closely with these auxiliary units during his military career, no more so than during the invasion of Britain. It is to that campaign the next chapter will turn to in detail.

Summary

Vespasian had risen from a minor equestrian family to the heady heights of the senate. Nothing up to then had suggested that he was destined for ultimate power. He was merely one among hundreds of senators. Yet he now had an opportunity under Claudius to show his military prowess, placed in charge of one of the four legions in an army numbering over 20,000 men led by General Plautius. A similar number of auxiliary units accompanied them. Vespasian was to play a major role in several battles and lead a major campaign westward. But on the morning of the invasion nothing was certain. The men were nervous. Britain was a land of ghosts and magic. Some felt they had no business going beyond the borders of the known world.

Would they walk into disaster just as Varus did in Germania? Their fathers and grandfathers would have told them the horrors of what was inflicted on the captured Romans. Some even survived and made their way back to Rome with tales of bloody sacrifices and torture among the trees. Would their stay be as brief as Caesar's a century before? They may have heard of victorious battles but wondered why then did the great Caesar leave after just a few weeks?

Vespasian himself might have felt nervous. He was thirty-three years old. This campaign could make a political career, but it could also destroy one. It could end in defeat and death. But perhaps worse than that was the ignominy of failure before it even started. In fact, disaster nearly struck before it began. The men refused to board the ships. Was Claudius about to be humiliated as Caligula had been on the beaches of northern Gaul? With an army refusing their emperor's orders, scared of what lay beyond the known world. The invasion hung in the balance.

Chapter 3

THE INVASION OF BRITAIN

Before we turn to the Claudian invasion, it is worth looking at the previous Roman experience with Britain. Nearly a century before, in 56 BC, Julius Caesar had conquered much of Gaul. It had taken two years of hard fighting. As the winter months drew in, he considered the threat from the mysterious island a short distance from the Gallic coast. Caesar claimed tribes from the island had assisted the Gauls in their resistance against Roman expansion, although he made no mention of specific aid when describing campaigns against northern Gallic tribes such as the Veneti. Decades of trading links may have led the Romans to suspect rich mineral resources lay within easy reach. They were certainly aware of the tin trade from the south-west peninsula. However, it was propably the lure of glory and glamour in leading a Roman army to unexplored lands that was a major motivation for the invasion, especially lands across the sea and on the edge of the known world.

As the campaigning season drew to a close, Caesar moved south and wintered in Cisalpine Gaul as he finalised plans. An early crossing the following year would give Caesar many months to achieve his aims in Britain. However, in the spring events intervened. Two Germanic tribes, the Usipetes and Tencteri, crossed the Rhine and raided into Gaul. Towns were burnt, people killed and slaves and loot taken.

Caesar marched north immediately to deal with the threat. Weighed down by plunder, the barbarians were intercepted before they could escape over the Rhine. The Romans quickly defeated them. Not wishing to leave a threat to his rear he delayed the invasion. Instead, Caesar decided to make a lightning raid into Germania. In a remarkable feat of engineering, a bridge was quickly built, allowing a punitive expedition. He marched a force across the river and laid waste to the surrounding region. Just eighteen days later his army was back across the Rhine and the bridge dismantled.

By late summer of 55 BC he was ready. It was an enormous risk to campaign so late. If they stayed too long bad weather might keep them in Britain over winter. Such a situation might prove fatal if the army could not be supplied or forage for food and water. But Caesar often gambled and this time was no exception. Two legions accompanied him, the Seventh and the Tenth. Caesar sent Caius Volusenus ahead to scout a suitable landing spot. Five days later, Volusenus returned and the fleet of warships and a hundred transports made ready, most likely from modern Boulogne. Eighty of the transports would be filled with infantry, perhaps 100 per vessel, with a further eighteen set aside for cavalry.[1]

The Britons were well aware of Roman intentions and had sent envoys to Gaul to discuss alliances and offer hostages. Caesar sent a Gallic chieftain, Commius, former king of the Atrebates, back across the channel. Time dragged on, yet no word came back. Unknown to the Romans, Commius had been imprisoned as soon as he stepped ashore. It was late August and Caesar could wait no longer. The order was given and the ships inched out of the harbour just before dawn.

By late morning the infantry transports had sighted the coast. This appears to have been near Dover as we read of cliffs lined by warriors. Caesar waited at anchor a few hours for all his available ships to arrive. The cavalry transports had been late departing and bad weather prevented them proceeding. Caesar waited as long as he could but eventually decided to continue without his cavalry. Another gamble. He pressed on, advancing about seven miles up the coast. Eventually a suitable landing spot was found, possibly near Deal or Walmer in eastern Kent. Unencumbered by high cliffs, a wide beach offered the best prospect for a successful assault.

The Britons had other ideas and made ready to throw the invaders back into the sea. Then, near disaster for the Romans. The transports could not get close enough, many grounding, some a long way off the beach. The legionaries had to jump into the sea and wade ashore, carrying their equipment. Chariots and cavalry were able to pick off the Romans with missiles and cut down stragglers as they came ashore. Caesar ordered his warships in close to provide covering fire from artillery, slings and archers.

They raked the shore with deadly fire from arrows, ballista bolts and stones. One can imagine the shock for any unfamiliar with such weapons. One second your friend is by your side, shield and spear in hand. The next an iron bolt throws him back several feet, dead before he hits the ground. A man holds a bloody stump where a stone has ripped a limb. Another has a crushed skull, victim of an onager.

But the legionaries were struggling to form a line to fight, let alone gain a foothold. The entire enterprise hung in the balance. The faltering Roman line was being driven back into the sea. Caesar himself tells us that it was the actions of a single man that helped to turn the tide of battle. The eagle-bearer of the Tenth Legion took a fateful decision. Seeing his comrades on the beach being struck down, and those around him reluctant to join the battle, he bravely jumped down from his ship and into the surf. Sadly, the man's name is lost to history.

The legionary exhorted the men to follow him:[2] 'Leap down, soldiers, unless you wish to betray your eagle to the enemy; it shall be told that I at any rate did my duty to my country and my general.' He waded towards the beach alone, holding the eagle aloft. Waiting for him were the Britons, jubilant in their expectation of victory. The legionaries could not bear the disgrace of losing their legionary eagle. Men started to jump in after him. An initial trickle turned into a flood as more and more of his comrades followed. Those in the ships nearest seeing what was happening did likewise.

The eagle-bearer made the beach and was joined by others. They formed a ragged line. The line held and was strengthened as more legionaries came ashore. The Britons, relying on cavalry and chariots, more suited to hit-and-run tactics, were unable to hold a position or make a strong defensive formation. Their assaults began to falter. Instead of easy pickings of isolated legionaries, what faced them now was a wall of wood and iron. They wheeled away to fight another day. The Romans took the beach, drove off the remaining Britons and constructed a camp. Local tribes were cowed enough to offer hostages and grain, and Commius was released. First blood was to Caesar. Just.

Four days later, the ships carrying the cavalry finally arrived off the coast. Once more, near disaster struck again. The Romans must have wondered whose side the gods were on when a storm drove off the precious cavalry transports. Worse, twelve of their infantry transports were destroyed and many others damaged. The Romans, heartened by their initial victory, were now in some disarray. Cavalry aside, if they could not repair their ships quickly, they might be trapped in Britain over winter.

The allied chieftains sensed an opportunity and quietly slipped out of the camp. The promised grain supply was cut. The Britons regrouped and prepared for war. The Romans were forced to forage for food. Units were ambushed by chariots and cavalry. A deadly game of cat and mouse played out across the fields of east Kent. This time the Romans were the mouse, scampering out of their hole to find crumbs of food. One group was caught in the open and on the verge of annihilation. Messages were sent back and Caesar personally led two cohorts, 1,000 men, to the rescue.

Caesar's personal bravery is well-documented.[3] As a young man he risked his life standing up to Sulla's command to divorce Cornelia, even after financial punishments and a clear threat of execution. He had received the *corona civica*, the highest awards for gallantry and bravery, when Mitylene on Lesbos was stormed.

Caesar led his relatively small force into unknown territory against an unknown number of enemy. This is likely within a day's march of the camp on the east coast of Kent. Once again, his gamble and personal bravery paid off. Caesar's two cohorts rescued the beleaguered men and retreated back to camp.

The Britons followed, harassing them all the way, no doubt believing they had the Romans boxed in. But they had underestimated their opponent. Rather than wait for a long siege or enemy reinforcements, Caesar lead his men outside the camp and formed up, flanked by a troop of cavalry provided by Commius and his allies. In an open field with room to manoeuvre the Romans were at an advantage. Now it was the Britons' turn to be the mouse and they were lured into the fight. Roman discipline told and they were beaten off, badly enough to sue for peace. Caesar demanded double the number of hostages to accompany him to Gaul.

The invasion was presented as a triumph by Caesar but, in reality, he was in Britain just a few weeks, barely advancing into the interior. The manner of leaving may indicate just how precarious his position was. Fearing a turn in the weather, he crammed his entire army onto the sixty-eight remaining transports and left at midnight around the September equinox. Two of the ships grounded in northern Gaul and were attacked by the Morini. Caesar had to send his cavalry to rescue the men.

No doubt many Britons felt that they had bloodied the Romans' nose and driven Caesar back across the sea with his tail between his legs. Caesar would claim he had crossed to an unknown land, won a battle and taken hostages. The Romans lapped up the news and the Senate awarded him twenty days of public thanksgiving. But Caesar had not finished with Britain. He spent the winter plotting a return.

The second invasion 54 BC

This time the Romans were better prepared. Six hundred transport ships were built, with oars and sails, and twenty-eight new war galleys. A further 200 transports were chartered from local tribes and added to the surviving ships from the year before. Five legions were accompanied by half of Caesar's available auxiliaries and cavalry.[4]

On 6 July the Roman fleet set off. Low winds slowed them but the oarsmen made steady progress and by noon they were at the landing beach. The new ships allowed men and horses straight onto the beach which was secured unopposed. It is thought that he landed close to the same site as the previous year. A marching camp has been found, 20 hectares in size, at Ebbsfleet near Pegwell Bay in East Kent just over six miles north of Deal. It was large enough to accommodate two legions and had a defensive ditch five metres wide and two metres deep.[5] The ships probably anchored in the Wantsum Channel, which, in Roman times, was up to two miles wide and sheltered by the Isle of Thanet to the west.

The Britons had formed up on the high ground but if they had hoped for an easy victory, at the sight of the size of the Roman force in front of them they reconsidered and retreated. Caesar meant business. He left ten cohorts and 300 cavalry to guard the camp and marched out at night with forty cohorts and 1,700 cavalry. The 20,000 legionaries covered twelve miles, half a day's march for a Roman soldier, and found the Britons waiting for them behind a river. It must still have been morning, and the river was probably the Stour near Canterbury. A larger force of Britons occupied a walled enclosure on a wooded hill, possibly Bigbury Wood hillfort.

Cavalry and chariots attacked from the fort but were brushed aside by Roman cavalry. The Romans built a ramp up to the wall and legionaries from the Seventh used *testudo* formation to storm the fort. Shields interlocked above and on the sides, the well-drilled soldiers inched up the man-made ramp. The Britons, initially feeling safe behind their earthworks, had probably never experienced such a sight. They fled, allowing the Romans to take the stronghold. Securing their position they rested for the night. Next morning, three columns were sent out to seek the enemy. Once again, the weather intervened.

A storm developed and back at the beach forty ships were destroyed. Many others were damaged. Caesar recalled the columns which must have been hugely frustrating after their initial victory. The Romans lost ten days dragging the ships ashore, enlarging the beachhead and making repairs. Messages were sent back to Gaul requesting craftsmen to repair the damaged ships.

Meanwhile the Britons had re-organised, appointing a certain Cassivellaunus as their leader. It is thought he came from the Catuvellauni tribe, north of the Thames. The Britons began harassing the Romans with hit-and-run tactics and ambushes. Caesar tells of a major attack as the Romans constructed a camp after a long day's march. A tribune was killed, and Caesar had to send two cohorts to reinforce and drive off the Britons. Foraging parties were constantly ambushed but Caesar pressed on, aiming for the homeland of the enemy chieftain. This meant crossing the Thames, a formidable barrier at the time.

The site of the subsequent engagement is disputed. Previously, some believed it to have been close to present day London. However, the lowest fordable point in Roman times was at Tilbury, opposite Gravesend and Northfleet in north-west Kent.[6] Here was the territory of the Trinovantes tribe. Caesar tells us sharpened stakes had been placed below the water line and along the northern bank. The Romans brought in their war-galleys to strafe the defenders with ballistae, slingers and archers. Engineers removed sections of the stakes as infantry and cavalry forded the river. A simultaneous attack drove the Britons off. The Romans had gained a foothold across the last major barrier into the heart of enemy territory.

The Britons conducted a scorched-earth policy, destroying farms and driving away livestock ahead of the Roman advance. Foraging parties were subject to heavy losses and up to 4,000 enemy chariots harried Caesar's troops. Caesar had experience in Gaul and was as well-used to diplomacy as the battlefield. Envoys were sent out to divide the tribes. The Trinovantes surrendered and five other tribes followed quickly. They told Caesar where the main settlement of Cassivellaunus was located. This *oppida*, a large fortified Iron Age settlement, lay in a heavily wooded area protected by marshes to the north west.

One possibility is Wheathampstead in Hertfordshire, the location of which can be seen in figure 13. The defences are still visible today: 30 metres wide and 12 metres deep. The Romans wasted no time. Ballistae and slingers swept the earthworks as the Romans, again using the *testudo* formation, attacked on two sides. The stronghold fell and significant resources were captured, including a large number of cattle. Back at the main camp in Kent a large-scale attack by local tribes was repelled and the Britons suffered major losses.

This time Caesar could legitimately claim a victory. By the end of September Cassivellaunus sued for peace. Commius of the Atrebates was again central to negotiations. It was claimed an annual tribute was agreed along with hostages and a promise not to attack the Trinovantes. This is important to note as it provides a possible pretext for later Roman policy towards Britain. Perhaps the victory was not as complete as Caesar claimed, given the manner of the withdrawal, although not quite as rushed as the year before.

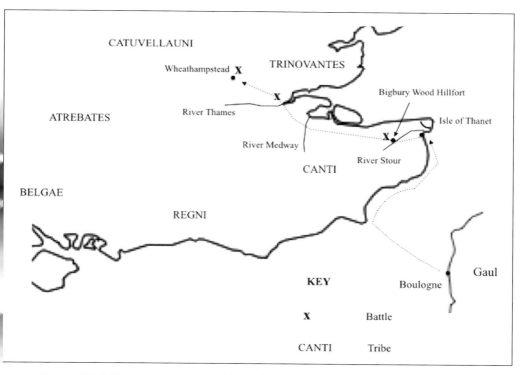

Figure 13: Julius Caesar's second invasion 54 BC.

Eager to return to Gaul before bad weather set in, and with ships still damaged, he decided to make two crossings. This meant splitting his forces and waiting for the ships to return. The first crossing went smoothly but poor weather made Caesar and his remaining men wait several days. He was in the position of being stranded over winter with half his force and fearing an attack. The returning ships failed to materialise. Once again, he risked a nighttime dash, with men rammed into the remaining ships. His luck held and by dawn they had sighted the coast of Gaul.

Trade with Britain increased, shifting markedly eastwards to Kent. It is not known if tribute was ever paid but Gaul at least evolved into a thoroughly Roman province. Just over a decade later, in 44 BC, Julius Caesar was assassinated and Rome lurched into civil war. The result of those upheavals was the end of the republic and the birth of the empire. It was eighty years before the Romans returned to Britain and when they did Vespasian was one of the four legates watching the coast as it slid past the prow of the ship.

Claudius and the invasion of Britain

Tiberius Claudius Nero Germanicus was born at Lugdunum in Gaul in 10 BC, the youngest son of Drusus the Elder, brother to Emperor Tiberius. His older brother, Germanicus, had an illustrious military career, married into the imperial family (a daughter of Tiberius's second wife) and was adopted by the emperor, becoming the natural heir to the throne. A favourite of the people, the older Germanicus unfortunately died in AD 19. Many suspected foul play. Tiberius ruled a further eighteen years and was succeeded by the son of Germanicus and nephew to the future conqueror of Britain.

Caligula was to rule for less than four years and the sources, kind to him at the start of his reign, widely condemned his cruelty and recklessness. His assassination led to the ascension of his uncle, an event even his closest family viewed with concern. Claudius had grown up during the reigns of Augustus, Tiberius and Caligula but held no notable civic or military posts. A sickly child, his condition had dulled 'both his mind and his body'.[7] His own mother, Antonia, called him 'a monster of a man, not finished but merely begun' and when insulting others would say they were 'a bigger fool than my son Claudius'.

When learning of his ascension his sister Livilla 'openly and loudly prayed' that Rome would be spared her brother's rule. Suetonius quotes a letter from Augustus discussing the 'Claudius problem'. Was he fit for public office? Was he 'defective in soundness of body and mind'? How could they avoid the potential ridicule and embarrassment? It was only under Caligula that Claudius gained an important role, serving as co-consul.

Somehow Claudius had survived the machinations of Roman politics, mainly by being widely dismissed as a non-entity and unthreatening figure, often the butt of ridicule. The invasion of Britain very nearly didn't happen as there was an abortive attempt on his life in 42 and at least six further attempts during the rest of his reign.[8] Scribonianus had revolted in Dalmatia but his legions refused to support the coup, earning them the title *Claudia Pia Fidelis* ('Claudius' own, loyal and true').

This was not the first time Rome had cast its eyes across the ocean since the invasions of Caesar. Part of the alleged agreement was that the Catuvellauni would not invade the Trinovantes. By the reign of Tiberius, the Catuvellaunian king, Cunobelin, had made the Trinovantian capital, Camulodunum, modern Colchester, his base, but maintained a friendly relationship with Rome. Perhaps this was a political marriage and continued good relations, and possibly tribute, prevented Roman retribution.

However, as it turned out, Cunobelin's sons were to play a major role in the Claudian invasion. One son, Adminius, fled to Rome during the reign of Caligula seeking help. His brothers, Caratacus and Togodumnus, had a very different attitude towards Rome from their brother or father. When their father died, they attacked Verica, a king of Atrebates, an ally of Rome, setting themselves on a collision course with the Empire.

Rome had come close to invading several times after Caesar's expeditions.[9] Augustus called off a planned invasion as early as 34 BC due to a Dalmatian revolt and again in c. 27 BC due to unrest in Gaul. Two centuries later Cassius Dio writes that Augustus had set out for Britain. He lingered in Gaul to deal with civil wars amongst the subjugated tribes and then it seems the Britons agreed terms.[10] The Britons reneged two years later but this time a revolt in Spain prevented action. It is possible this marks the cessation of the tribute payments agreed by Caesar.

Augustus wrote in *Res Gestae Divi Augustus*, 'The Deeds of the Divine Augustus', that two British kings requested aid: Tincommius of the Atrebates and Dubnovellaunus of the Trinovantes. Both had come under pressure from the Catevellauni a few decades before the actions of Caratacus and Togodumnus precipitated the Claudian invasion.

Strabo, writing during the reign of Augustus, provides an interesting clue as to the treaty arrangements that may have existed. British chieftains had sent embassies and dedicated offerings and we read that they had 'made the island Roman'. What though does this mean? It may be a reference to the heavy taxes imposed on imports and exports. The Britons were so subdued, according to Strabo, that there was no need to garrison the island. In fact, only 'one legion, at the least, and some cavalry would be required in order to carry off tribute from them, and the expense of the army would offset the tribute-money'. This may reflect the position before the emperor's aborted invasion or possibly after a new agreement had been reached. Frustratingly there are gaps in the evidence. We have no record of any planned interventions in Britain under Tiberius but Caligula also famously planned an expedition.

It was during his reign that the Catevellaunian prince, Adminius, had quarrelled with his father, Cunobelin, and fled to Gaul. Caligula spied an opportunity and prepared a fleet. The army was already disgruntled with a reduction in pay and the dismissal of generals and long serving centurions. A farcical campaign in Germania did little to boost morale. A fleet was prepared and the army brought to the northern coast of Gaul.

But the army was reluctant. They had heard tales of ghosts and cannibals. Strange monsters inhabited the forests and mists. Caligula was outraged and drew up his men on the beach. Ballistae and artillery faced the sea. Some probably feared reprisals but the emperor's next actions surprised them. He sailed past on a trireme and then disembarked to sit on a platform overlooking the assembled troops. They were ordered to gather shells, filling their helmets and the folds of their tunics and cloaks. These he sent to Rome with claims that he had enslaved the ocean. The official 'surrender' of Adminius was used to bolster claims that he had subdued the Britons. He even held a triumph, parading 'captives' from his German campaign, many of whom were in fact deserters forced to dye their hair red and grow it long and dress in barbarian clothes.

Cassius Dio adds to the account of Suetonius: Caligula 'set out as if to conduct a campaign against Britain but turned back from the ocean's edge'.[11] The soldiers were drawn up on the beach while the emperor sailed past. Returning to the shore he sat on a 'lofty platform' and gave the order to collect sea-shells. Trumpeters urged them on as the proud legionaries scrambled about across the beach. Caligula we are told became 'greatly elated, as if he had enslaved the very ocean; and he gave his soldiers many presents'.

Within a year Caligula lay dead but his uncle inherited a fleet of transports which formed the core of the 900 the Romans would eventually use. Those ships would later evolve into the *Classis Britannica* regional fleet. Caligula had also erected a lighthouse, presumably at Gesoriacum, Boulogne, and expanded the port. The Britons must have mocked the antics of Caligula and laughed even louder when they heard about the new emperor and the descriptions of him. If they had known what was to happen, they would have urged the praetorian guardsman to strike down the cowering man found shaking with fear behind the palace curtains.

The invasion

The opportunity to use Caligula's fleet came quickly. The Catuvellaunian king, Cunobelin had died in late 40 and was succeeded by his sons Caratacus and Togodumnus. Perhaps it was Caligula's death and news that Rome was in turmoil and governed by a weak, elderly emperor that prompted them. They attacked the Atrebates in the Thames valley. Their king, Verica, fled to Rome where he found a sympathetic ear with the new emperor. Claudius, already possessing the means, now had a motive.

Suetonius adds a slightly different reason stating Claudius sought an imperial triumph and chose Britain as the best place for gaining it.[12] The Britons were 'in a state of rebellion because of the refusal to return certain deserters'. Whatever the primary cause, the immediate objective was probably returning friendly client kings to power in tribes along the southern coast.

Strabo, writing a generation before, had estimated just one legion and some cavalry could subdue the island but more was gained from customs than tribute.[13] Claudius had bigger things on his mind than economics. A successful campaign would cement his position and legacy. He placed Aulus Plautius in charge of four legions: Legio XIV Gemina, Legio XX Valera Victrix, Legio IX Hispana and Vespasian's Legio II Augusta. Auxiliary units and cavalry brought the total force up to about 40,000.

Liburnian bireme galleys, two banks or oars on each side, made ready alongside hundreds of transport ships. But, again, the troops were reluctant. The Britons were enormous, ferocious, blue-skinned savages beyond the borders of the known world. The days were sunless and filled with cold fog and rain. Plautius had great difficulty persuading his men to embark.

Eventually they were shamed into action. Tiberius Claudius Narcissus was a member of the emperor's advisory council, the *Consilium Principis*. The same man had gained Vespasian his position as legate of the Second Augusta. A former slave, he boarded the nearest ship shouting *Io Saturnalia!*, a reference to the role reversal performed at the end of year festival. The soldiers stirred, no doubt muttered curses, but reluctantly followed the former slave aboard.

Figure 15 shows a map of the empire just before Claudius came to power. The most likely landing spot for the invasion was Richborough near Pegwell Bay in East Kent, close to where Caesar had placed his main camp.[14] An alternative route via the south coast has not gained

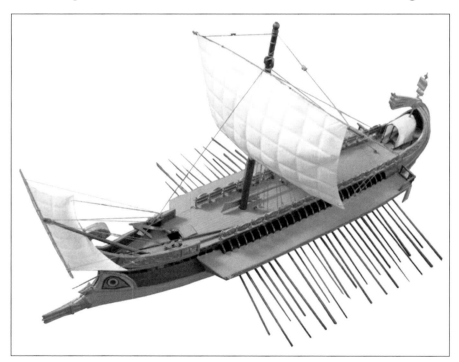

Figure 14: Model of Roman Trireme. (Wikimedia Commons)

support but both routes can be seen in figure 16. A grand monumental arch built by Domitian at Richborough, alongside archaeological evidence of ditch and bank fortifications, point to East Kent as being the main landing point.

The Romans were unopposed and quickly established a bridgehead. A speedy victory at the River Stour a few miles inland allowed them to build a fort. They pressed onwards but came to a major obstacle, very likely the Medway. On the far bank massed the Britons, led by Togodumnus and Caratacus. Cassius Dio states the Romans had landed in three divisions and caught the Britons ill-prepared.[15] Interestingly, we learn that the Romans 'gained by capitulation a part of the Dodunni, who were ruled by a tribe of the Catuellani'.

Dio could be mistaken here as the Dobunni were located in the Severn Valley. Alternatively, this might indicate a southern landing spot and a Roman force pushing north, securing their western flank. Or perhaps the Romans simply sent envoys to all the southern tribes.

Back at the Medway, Plautius faced a serious threat. The Britons were a considerable force, protected by a significant barrier. The defenders assumed they were safe, protected by the wide expanse of water, and

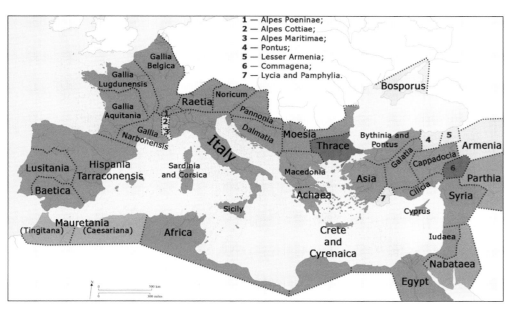

Figure 15: Map of Roman Empire under Caligula. (Wikimedia Commons)

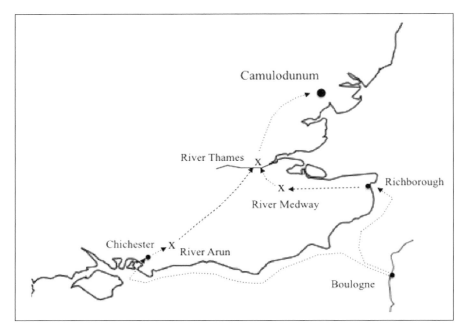

Figure 16: Map showing the possible invasion routes in AD 43.

camped on the western bank, spread out in a 'rather careless fashion'. But the Romans had a trick up their sleeves. A unit of Germanic auxiliaries, trained to swim in full armour, crossed the river. Ignoring the warriors they attacked the horses. That caused mass confusion and panic.

It was Vespasian's moment, accompanied by his brother Sabinus acting as his lieutenant. As Sabinus was also a senator, the implication here is that he led his own legion but Vespasian was in command of the operation. Plautius ordered the Second Legion to cross and it took the Britons by surprise. There are no details about how the Romans crossed – possibly a ford upstream or perhaps by boat in a navigable part of the river downstream. Many Britons were killed and the Romans sensed victory. The enemy were not finished. They returned the next day and very nearly succeeded in pushing Vespasian back across the river. The arrival of another legion led by Gnaeus Hosidius Geta won the day, an action for which Geta received the *ornamenta triumphalia*.

The Britons retreated, but it had been a close-run thing and they lived to fight another day. Plautius followed hot on their heels. As with Caesar's second invasion, the Britons reached the Thames which at the time was much wider. The Britons knew the safe paths across at low tide, but the Romans were forced to stop. Dio describes the place as follows: 'a point near where it empties into the ocean and at flood-tide forms a lake. This they easily crossed because they knew where the firm ground and the easy passages in this region were to be found.'

Once again, the Germanic auxiliaries swam across whilst the legionaries crossed via a bridge a little way upstream, suggesting they had time to construct one. Perhaps this was a quick pontoon bridge made by lashing ships together. As with Caesar, the exact crossing point is unknown although Tilbury as the lowest fordable point is likely.[16] The Thames today is about fifteen feet higher than at the time of the invasion.[17] Plautius would have looked out across mud flats interspersed with freshwater streams which shifted and changed course as the tides came and went.

The Britons, attacked by Germanic auxiliaries emerging from the river and from legionaries on their flank, began to break. Unable to stand against the Roman military machine they retreated. Some legionaries made the fatal mistake of pursuing them through the swamps. Many that weren't drowned were ambushed and the Romans lost a significant number of men. But the day was theirs and they made camp on the north bank of the river. Togodumnus died soon after this second battle, possibly from wounds. Caratacus became the sole commander and would be a thorn in the Romans' side for years to come.

The Romans were expert engineers and a bridge across the Medway, or later the Thames, was well within their capability. This could have been a simple matter of a pontoon bridge, or ships lashed together. However, they were capable of much grander engineering projects and at remarkable speed too. This was shown by Caesar's lightning raid into Germania in 55 BC, just months before his first invasion of Britain.[18]

He crossed the Rhine at Coblenz where today the river is about 400 yards wide and averages 5 to 25 feet in depth. A timber bridge 36-feet wide, about 11 metres, was constructed. Working from rafts, pairs of timbers, eighteen-inches thick, were rammed into the riverbed, angled in the direction of the flow. About 40 feet to the side, another pair were set, forming trestles between which joists, two-feet thick, were connected. The trestles were placed at intervals across the river as the thick joists allowed a platform to be created, strong enough to accommodate the legions and cavalry. Further piles were placed in front of the bridge to protect from 'trunks of trees, or vessels, … launched by the natives to break down the structure'.

All this took just ten days to cut down and prepare what must have been a vast amount of timber. Caesar spent a little of two weeks burning villages and destroying crops whilst the German tribes sensibly took their people deep into the forests. Just eighteen days later, Caesar was back across the Rhine in Gaul. The bridge was dismantled, leaving nothing behind that the Germanic tribes could use.

In contrast the Thames near Tilbury today is about 500 yards at its narrowest but in the first century it was about fifteen feet lower.[19] In the first century, the river may have been narrower at low tide; however, at high tide, swamps, tidal pools and shifting sands made the paths across difficult and ever changing. The determining factor would have been time. A pursuit, followed by a quick assault, which seems the most likely scenario, required a rapid crossing. Thus, it may be more likely that the Romans lashed their boats together to form a pontoon bridge. But we cannot dismiss the possibility that one was built, or that they used a wooden causeway that was already there.

Plautius prepared for an advance on the Catuvellaunian capital at Camulodunum. If we trust Cassius Dio, apparently Plautius 'became afraid, and instead of advancing any farther, proceeded to guard what he had already won sending for Claudius.' It is at this point that we get the first mention of elephants in the campaign, 'For he had been instructed to do this in case he met with any particularly stubborn resistance, and, in fact, extensive equipment, including elephants, had already been got together for the expedition'.[20]

The emperor, we are told, took command and won a great victory at Camulodunum, winning over many tribes, 'in some cases by capitulation, in others by force'. He was 'saluted as *imperator* several times … deprived the conquered of their arms and handed them over to Plautius.' Leaving his general to subjugate the remaining districts, he hastened back to Rome. His sons-in-law, Magnus and Silanus, were sent ahead. In Rome the senate honoured Plautius with the title *Britannicus*.

The emperor was away from Rome for six months, spending only sixteen days in Britain, little time to march on Camulodunum and conduct a successful campaign. It seems far more likely that Claudius had been waiting at Gesoriacum for word from Plautius that the situation was under control and that he simply entered the capital at his leisure.

There he would accept the surrender of eleven kings, the names of which were inscribed on a triumphal arch in Rome.[21]

It is likely the emperor congratulated the four legionary commanders personally. Whether this was at Camulodunum or the main camp north of the Thames is not known. Plautius did not sit on his hands. He had plans for the Second Legion and clearly trusted Vespasian to lead a campaign on his own. Before we turn to that it would be useful to look at the *oppidum* at Camulodunum in greater detail as it will indicate the type of settlement Vespasian was tasked to capture.

Camulodunum

The Romans described the main urban settlements they encountered as *oppidum* (plural *oppida*), meaning 'enclosed space'. Julius Caesar named twenty-eight in Gaul. These were centres of economic or political power. Strabo, referring specifically to Britain, stated, 'The forests are their cities; for they fence in a spacious circular enclosure with trees which they have felled, and in that enclosure make huts for themselves and also pen up their cattle.'[22] Caesar also described them:[23] Concealing themselves in the woods, the Britons fortified the approaches by 'a great number of felled trees'. The stronghold of Cassivellaunus was 'fenced by woods and marshes.'[24] In general the Britons fortified 'thick-set woodland with rampart and trench'.

Outside those strongholds, the Britons tended to live in farmsteads, often enclosed by an outer ditch and wall.[25] Roundhouses with thatched roofs, wattle-and-daub walls and timber posts were the norm. Large farmsteads had a number of such buildings, often for an extended multi-generational family group. One example found at Stansted in north-west Essex had eleven such round buildings within a square enclosure.[26]

Figures 17 and 18 portray examples of typical roundhouses from this period. These are from Castell Henllys Iron-Age Village in West Wales, a small hill fort that was probably abandoned before the Roman advance into southern Wales. However, they give a good idea of the type of small farmstead Vespasian would have encountered in 43. The first-century Briton, here portrayed by Owain Edwards, has distinctive blue patterns on his face and wears clothes typical of his era.

The Iron Age settlement at Camulodunum was well chosen, protected by two rivers on three sides. the Colne to the north and east and the

Figure 17: Re-enactment of 1st century Briton (Owain Edwards) outside roundhouse at Castell Henllys Iron-Age Village, Wales.

Figure 18: Reconstruction of typical first-century roundhouses at Castell Henllys Iron-Age Village, Wales.

Roman to the south. Earthworks defended the western gap between the rivers. Eastern earthworks protected against attack from the east across the Colne. The name is fought to derive from a Brythonic Celtic name, *Camulodunon*, meaning 'the stronghold of Camulus', the British god of war. The area between the earthworks and rivers was a massive 1,000 hectares, nearly four square miles. If the earthworks are included it was even larger, ten square miles between the valleys of the Colne and Roman.[27]

In comparison, modern Heathrow airport covers 1,227 hectares. It is likely that farmsteads and other buildings were spread out within the *oppidum*. This was much larger than the site at Wheathampstead, which was only 35 hectares. The later Roman town at Camulodunum covered just 43 hectares, demonstrating just how huge the pre-Roman site was. The dykes themselves measured twelve miles if placed end to end. They consisted of a V-shaped ditch with a bank behind. The largest ditches were thirteen metres deep with a similar sized bank rising behind it which would have proved extremely difficult for cavalry and impenetrable for chariots.

The settlement can be dated to c. 25 BC with coins from c. 10-15 BC.[28] There is no way of knowing if the site was in existence during Caesar's invasion, but that seems fairly likely. Evidence of a large high-status building within a farmstead has been found at Gosbecks to the southwest of the site. This was also a large high-status building believed to be home to a chieftain. A large square enclosure was surrounded by a deep, wide ditch.

To the north the Sheepen site area suggests extensive iron and leather working economic activity. A port gave access to the river. Coins found there depict sailing vessels, the only known ones from iron-age Britain. Imported pottery and amphorae imply significant levels of trade.

Within the settlement was a landscape of pasture, cultivated fields and woodland. Crops such as wheat, barley, oats, peas and beans were grown, Livestock was predominantly cattle but pigs, sheep and goats were also common. The first fort may have been built to the west, in an area protected on all sides by the river and earthworks. The first legionary fort was built farther east against the Colne but a smaller auxiliary fort has been found south-west of the site.

Camulodunum has claim to be Britain's oldest recorded town or even Britain's first city. Pliny mentions it in his *Natural history*:[29]

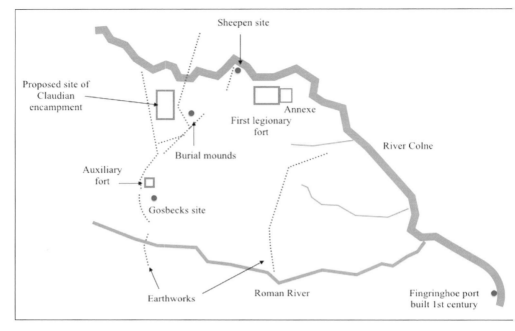

Figure 19: Camulodunum: Map of the Iron Age settlement and the first Roman fort.

'in Mona [Anglesey], which is about 200 miles from Camelodunum, a town of Britain'. A second-century inscription in Rome gives the name as '*colonia Victricensis* which is at Camulodunum in Britannia …' (*coloniae Victricensis quae est in Brittannia Camaloduni*). Tacitus claimed it was founded in 49: 'a colony was settled on conquered lands at Camulodunum by a strong detachment of veterans, who were to serve as a bulwark against revolt and to habituate the friendly natives to their legal obligations.'[30] By 61, the year of the Boudican revolt, Colchester (a *colonia*) and St Albans (a *municipium*) were chartered Roman towns. London was a mere trading post.

An auxiliary fort was built first, near the Sheepen site, but this was followed by a legionary fortress constructed very soon after the invasion, c. 43-4.[31] This was initially garrisoned by the Twentieth Legion. To the east a large annexe was built. In c. 48 the Twentieth was sent westwards to chase down the elusive Caratacus, then fighting with the Silures in South Wales. It was at this point that a new *colonia* of retired veterans was established. The fortress was abandoned and the defences levelled with the ditches filled in. This was to prove a disastrous decision a decade later. Crucially the new town was 'unprotected by fortifications'.[32] Just over a decade later it was destroyed by Boudica. The town was rebuilt and became the modern Colchester.

Summary

Back in 43 Plautius no doubt breathed a sigh of relief after the emperor's flying visit. The campaign had already achieved more than Caesar's two invasions. A new province was being carved out of the south-east of the island. Tribal kings were swearing allegiance and those still resisting had fled to the west and north. There was still work to do. Vespasian received his orders from the general. He was heading westwards deep into enemy territory with a single legion. As Plautius secured the south-east, Vespasian gathered his legionaries and auxiliary units. The next chapter details Vespasian's campaign across southern Britain.

Chapter 4

VESPASIAN'S CAMPAIGN IN SOUTHERN BRITAIN

Suetonius tells us that Vespasian fought thirty battles, and reduced to subjection 'two powerful nations, more than twenty towns (*oppida*), and the island of Vectis'[1], the last being the Isle of Wight. Who were these warlike tribes and where were these twenty *oppida?* Plautius remained in the south-east of Britain, securing what was to become a new province. Verica, king of the Atrebates, and Cogidubnus of the Regni were both friendly towards Rome. We can thus rule out the first two tribes to the west of the Canti as possible opponents. The Isle of Wight, the first potentially hostile territory Vespasian would have encountered, was an ideal staging point for a campaign west.

Plautius had sent Vespasian to secure the southern coast and his western flank before he pushed into the interior of the island. We recall that the Dobunni along the east bank of the Severn surrendered early in the campaign. One possible candidate for the first of those hostile tribes was the Belgae, centred on what was to become Winchester, *Venta Belgarum*. Further west, the territory of the Dumnonii of Devon and Cornwall was not compromised until the 50s with a legionary fortress established at Exeter in c. 55.[2] It thus seems certain that the Durotriges, in modern Dorset, were one of the 'two powerful nations'.

Lying between the Belgae and Dumnonii, the Durotriges may have been the greater threat. Over fifty hill-forts were spread across their territory in southern England. South Cadbury, Spettisbury Rings, Hod Hill and Maiden Castle have all shown evidence of assaults alongside massacres of the defenders.[3]

At South Cadbury the remains of thirty men, women and children appear to have been left to rot although their injuries could have been caused by animals.[4] Radio-carbon dating of charred wood gave a date range of 45-61, so it could just as easily be due to Boudicca's revolt rather than Vespasian's campaign.

At Hod Hill it appears that the defenders attempted to strengthen the defences before abandoning it halfway through.[5] A new outer ditch ends suddenly for no apparent reason. Inside the fort we find signs of the possible cause, fifteen *ballista* bolts, seemingly directed at the chieftain's hut. The Romans must have occupied the area as a Roman fort was built into the north-west corner. The best evidence lies at Maiden Castle which will be detailed below.

We can see one suggested route of Vespasian's campaign in the map in figure 20. Just four of the many scores of hill-forts in this part of the country are noted: Maiden Castle, Spettisbury Rings, Hod Hill and South Cadbury. Assaulting a hill-fort was no easy task. The defences were formidable.

We have two contemporary accounts of battles in the open field between Britons and Romans from the first century. Both are useful in demonstrating the type of engagement Vespasian might have experienced. The first is the battle of Walling Street c. 61. This was just eighteen years after Vespasian fought and so would have been a familiar experience. Titus served in Britain as a tribune shortly after this battle. It is not known which legion he was in, but it is likely he served with men who had had been present.

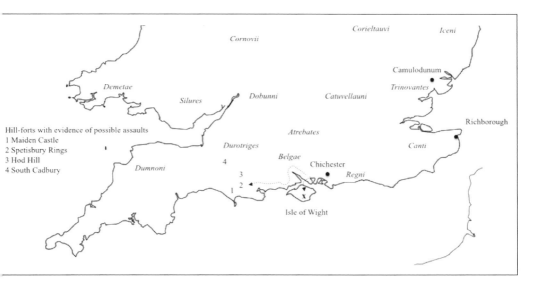

Figure 20: Map of Vespasian's campaign in the west.

Boudicca's revolt in c. 60 resulted in the destruction of Colchester, London and St Albans. An initial relief force was destroyed. When Gaius Suetonius Paulinus, governor of Roman Britain, heard the news, he was campaigning against the stronghold of the druids in northern Wales, on Mona, the island of Anglesey. He rushed back in a south-easterly direction with detachments of the Twentieth Legion and auxiliaries numbering 10,000 men. Somewhere along the route, presumably towards London, he met with a vast army of Britons. Sources claim that the force facing him was as high as 230,000, although this is considered an exaggeration by most historians. What seems certain is that the Romans were outnumbered vastly.

Tacitus provides further details:[6] The Romans chose their position well. Protected in the rear and flanks by woods, they took up a defensive position which could be approached only by a narrow pass. The heavily-armed legionaries formed in close ranks. To their sides were the lightly-armed troops and the infantry formation was flanked by cavalry. The Britons deployed in 'bands of foot and horse … moving jubilantly in every direction'. Confident from their recent successes, Tacitus tells us they had brought 'even their wives to witness the victory', placing them in wagons to their rear on the plain which lay before the Roman front line. The fate of Roman Britain hung in the balance. The battle was about to begin.

If we are to believe Tacitus, Boudicca gave a rousing speech from her chariot. Riding between the clans she reminded them of the purpose, vengeance: 'as a woman of the people, her liberty lost, her body tortured by the lash, the tarnished honour of her daughters.' Had they not destroyed a legion, burned their towns? The gods were surely on their side and their revenge was just. Having destroyed a relief force, mauled the Ninth Legion and destroyed three major towns, the Britons would have been confident. Even more so when they compared their huge force with the much smaller Roman army facing them.

Paulinus gave similarly stirring words. The men should trust to their training. Treat with contempt the 'noise and empty menaces of the barbarians'. These Britons were 'more women than soldiers … unwarlike and unarmed, they would break immediately.' They formed up, using the woods to protect their flanks.

One gets a sense of a Shakespearean speech from Henry V's mouth at Agincourt: 'The fewer men, the greater share of honour … We few, we happy few, we band of brothers.' Tacitus places similar words in the mouth of Paulinus: 'it was but a few men who decided the fate of battles; and it would be an additional glory that they, a handful of troops, were gathering the laurels of an entire army.' The general then instructed his men to keep close order and discharge their javelins first. Then advance using shield boss and sword. They were to ignore the chance of plunder but advance steadily over the dead as they piled up.

The battle began. The Britons came on in one mass and, having exhausted their missiles, they charged. The Romans discharged their *pila*. Each *pilum* weighed on average between 0.9-2.3 kilograms. An estimate of 8,000 heavy infantry and auxiliary troops, carrying two *pila* at 1.5 kg each, results in 24 tonnes of iron and wood raining down on the advancing Britons. Archers, slingers and other missile troops added to the barrage. This would have had a devastating impact on the front ranks and severely disrupted the initial charge. Any warriors surviving that were met with a wall of wood and iron.

The large *scutum* shield protected the legionary from shin to chin and if one placed it on the ground and bent slightly only the eyes would be visible above the rim. The deadly *gladius* sword, after a quick movement to the side with the shield arm, could be thrust out from the hip into the abdomen of the enemy. Alternatively, a thrust over the top of the shield could deliver a potentially fatal wound to the head, face or upper torso. If the front ranks held, those in the rear could use spears or missile weapons to cause more damage. The use of good quality helmets meant that the turn of one's head would cause an enemy sword or spear thrust over the top of the *scutum* to slide off the curved surface of the helmet.

Armour also offered excellent protection from any slicing blows. Only a very determined thrust with a narrow point could hope to break through. Even then weapons tests have demonstrated *lorica segmentata* gave excellent protection. Chain-mail, *lorica hamata*, and scales, *lorica squamata*, could occasionally be compromised but only by a determined spear thrust. In general, armour worked exceptionally well, even hardened leather. Many of the Britons, however, would have been very vulnerable.

The Romans advanced. They used a wedge-like formation and cut into the Britons. As they advanced, any wounded enemy were despatched by rear ranks as they stepped over them. The cavalry joined the fray and 'with lances extended, broke a way through'. It seems that the Britons at Watling Street relied on a mass charge often used by Celtic and Germanic warriors of the time. This could prove devastating. Here we see what happens when it fails.

One imagines a large band of warriors charging down a narrow corridor. At the other end stand a handful of determined, well-armed and armoured, trained and disciplined troops, perhaps three abreast and four deep. The initial charge might well brush them aside. However, if the front ranks of the charging mob were to fall this would hamper the effect. Those reaching the defenders first would be met with a wall of wood and the thrusting iron of swords and spears. If the defenders didn't break, the attackers had nowhere to go. Those behind would press upon their backs. Those at the front would succumb to sword thrusts and fall, their own attacks falling helplessly on shields and helmets. the few getting through sliding off armour. Panic might set in. Those turning to escape would be even more vulnerable. Momentum is important. The defenders become the attackers and step forward at a steady pace, despatching stragglers and the fallen as they go.

At Watling Street the Britons broke. As they fled, they were hampered by their own wagons and families to their rear. Panic ensued. The Romans came on and showed no mercy. Tacitus claims 80,000 Britons died, including many of the women in the baggage train. The Romans only lost 400 men. Boudicca allegedly died by her own hand, having taken poison.

This battle was less than twenty years after Vespasian's march across southern Britain. We can see why the Britons often resorted to guerrilla tactics. It shows how Vespasian would have approached a battle in open field. No doubt it was something every legate yearned for.

The second battle that might be instructive occurred in c. 83, forty years after Vespasian's campaign in Britain and during the reign of his second son, Domitian. General Agricola had actually fought at Watling Street. Twenty years later he was governor of Britain, leading an army north into unknown territory. For a contemporary account we turn to Tacitus once more.

Agricola had marched north with approximately 15,000 legionaries, 8,000 auxiliaries and 3,000 cavalry. Confronting him were 30,000 Caledonians led by the chieftain Calgacus. Tacitus again puts words into a protagonist's mouth. In one of the best-known lines from antiquity, the Romans are described as 'robbers of the world' and

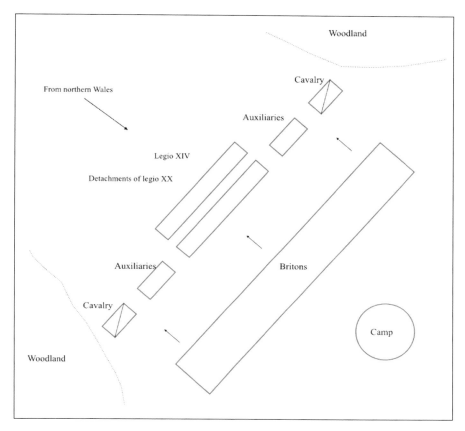

Figure 21: Battle of Watling Street c. 61.

'rapacious' with a 'lust for dominion'. Then: 'Alone among men they covet with equal eagerness poverty and riches. To robbery, slaughter, plunder, they give the lying name of empire; they make a solitude and call it peace.'[7]

Agricola held his heavy infantry, the 15,000 legionnaires, in reserve. His 8,000 auxiliaries formed a front line, flanked by cavalry. The Britons were formed up on the slope of a hill with their van on the plain in front. A screen of chariots and cavalry wheeled about between the two armies. The battle began.

Chariots and cavalry advanced on the Romans and delivered volleys of arrows and javelins. They had little effect. The Britons advanced with 'huge swords and small shields' and delivered 'a dense shower of darts' on the Romans. The swords the Britons carried are described as 'enormous … blunt at the point … unfit for close grappling, and engaging in a confined space'.

Agricola turned to his Germanic auxiliaries. Three Batavian and two Tungrian cohorts (approximately 2,500 men) advanced. The first major engagement occurred on the level ground at the base of the hill. The Britons were no match for the experienced battle-hardened Germans. Striking the Britons with the 'bosses of their shields and stabbing them in the face',[8] the Romans pushed their enemy up the slope of the hill. The remaining auxiliary cohorts joined the attack. A counter-attack using chariots was beaten off.

Still the Britons felt confident. They had the high ground and numerical advantage, certainly over this relatively small attacking force. They began to descend and tried to envelop the Roman advance. Agricola had been waiting for this and sent in four squadrons of horse to drive off the attempted flanking manoeuvre. This was successful and the Roman cavalry wheeled round to attack the flanks and rear of the Britons. The Britons found themselves pushed back by their own retreating men and a relentless advance by Germanic auxiliaries. Ominously, a wall of shields and swords came on up the hill. They were hit by cavalry in the sides and rear. The Britons broke and fled. A rearguard action some miles away blunted the pursuit but it was only nightfall and the impenetrable forest that eventually saved them from total destruction. Tacitus once again claims only 400 Roman dead. The Caledonians were said to have lost 10,000.

We can see maps of these two battles in figures 21 and 22. Figure 23 shows a typical battle formation of a first-century Roman legion accompanied by auxiliaries. The ten infantry cohorts of the legion would form up in two lines. The larger first cohort, consisting of 800 men, would hold the right flank. Next would come auxiliary troops. As we saw at Mons Graupius, these were formidable enough to win battles without the employment of the legions. In front would come the light troops and skirmishers. To the rear were archers, slingers and other missile troops, backed up by artillery: ballistae or scorpions. Cavalry would guard the flanks.

If Vespasian marched west with one of the four legions we can speculate that he took a quarter of the auxiliary troops as well. Ten auxiliary units would number around 5,000 troops. Perhaps two or three of those were cavalry units. There's no reason to suspect the Durotriges

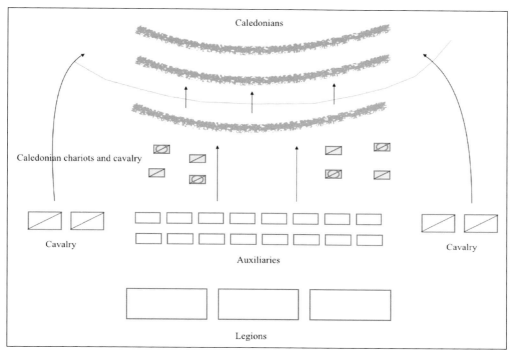

Figure 22: Battle of Mons Graupius c. 83.

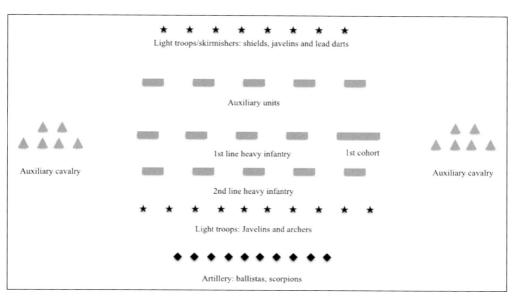

Figure 23: A typical Roman legion formation in the first century AD.

fared any better in open field than Boudicca or the Caledonians. With the Isle of Wight secure and the Britons unable to defeat the Romans in open battle the Romans marched west, supplied by their fleet hugging the southern coast. The Britons probably felt that the best option was to retreat to their hillforts. No doubt this had served them well in the past.

Whilst the Roman soldiers could march over twenty miles a day, the oxen pulling wagons were far slower, especially over rough ground. But those wagons brought inevitable defeat and death to the Britons. They carried artillery and siege weapons. The Romans also had people every bit has important to Roman victories: engineers and craftsmen, capable of building siege towers, ramps, bridges and tunnels. Some Britons might well have felt secure, looking down from behind their high earthen banks. Their initial smiles of relief would have turned to concern as they saw the Romans not attacking but surrounding their hill with earthworks and ramparts of their own. And what were those strange things they constructed and placed at intervals? If they had never seen such a machine in action, the shock must have been profound when the first stone or bolt smashed into a defender and sent body parts flying across the *oppidum*.

Maiden Castle

The *oppidum* at Maiden Castle was located two miles south-west of Dorchester in Dorset, deep within the territory of the Durotriges tribe. The largest iron-age hill fort in Europe, it covered 47 acres and stood 130 metres above sea level, 40 metres above the surrounding land. Built around 450-300 BC, the initial defences consisted of a V-shaped ditch and a rampart. To the south, four ramparts and three ditches were added and a fourth did not extend all the way round because of the steepness of the northern side. Further earthworks protected the eastern entrance. Entrances, protected by gates, were not aligned with gaps in the earthworks making assaults more difficult. Wooden palisades would have been built along the rampart.

The initial bank was 2.7 metres high overlooking a shallow ditch. However, Vespasian's men faced a much higher construction. A warrior standing at the bottom of the ditch had 8.4 metres, or nearly 30 feet, of earth in front of him, a formidable barrier, especially if topped with a wooden palisade defended by determined warriors able to rain down stones, spears and other missiles. Once you reached the top, tired after the climb, you would struggle to hold a shield above your head whilst wielding a sword or spear. It would be difficult even to stand upright and keep your footing. Today the ramparts still tower twenty feet above visitors.

A number of bodies of Iron Age warriors have been discovered during excavations. Some were buried with food and drink, possibly for their journey into the afterlife. Sir Mortimer Wheeler excavated the site in the 1930s and suggested that evidence showed men, women and children had been savagely killed with the few survivors left to bury the dead. One skull had a square piercing which looked like the result of a Roman ballista bolt. Another skeleton had an iron arrowhead still stuck in a vertebra. A large cut to the head of the same individual suggested an injured survivor had been put out of his misery. Three-quarters show evidence of violence from edged weapons or projectiles.

A large store of 40-50,000 sling stones taken from nearby Chesil Beach were also found during excavations, suggesting that the Britons could put up significant resistance.

Figure 24: Aerial view of Maiden Castle. (Wikimedia commons)

Figure 25: Ramparts at Maiden Castle. (Wikimedia commons)

Webster in *The Invasion of Roman Britain* provides further details.[9] Twenty-eight graves contained the bodies of twenty-three men and eleven women. Many had severe head injuries, and some showed signs of being hacked after death. The tops of the ramparts were deliberately pushed into the ditches and the gateways destroyed. The site then appeared to be abandoned. The nearby Roman town of Durnovaria became the modern town of Dorchester.

As formidable as these defences were, they proved no match against the Roman war machine. Vespasian would have surrounded the hillfort with a ring of death-delivering artillery, firing bolts and stones into the interior. One can only imagine the terror as the defenders huddled beneath whatever protection they could find. Those brave enough to look down on their foes would have stared in wonder as an earthen bank edged towards them across the first ditch and bank.

Slowly it extended its long arm as each bank was crossed in turn, Roman engineers working feverishly behind protective screens. Perhaps the last section was bridged with a wide gangplank. As it fell, legionaries poured over the bridge and into the settlement. Perhaps the defenders were confronted with a wall of shields as the attackers advanced in

Figure 26: Roman *testudo* formation from Trajan's Column. (Wikimedia commons)

testudo formation up the bank and over the wall, shields interlocked front, top and sides. We can see an example of this in figure 26 from Trajan's column.

Contemporary writers provide a vivid picture. From Plutarch, the first rank drops to one knee, shield in front with each rank protecting the head of the man in front, forming a roof. Dio describes its use in Mark Antony's Parthian campaign in 36 BC:[10] Ambushed by horse archers, they locked shields and protected themselves from the 'dense showers of arrows'. The Parthians, perhaps remembering the defeat of Crassus at Carrhae, dismounted and went in for the kill. That was a fatal mistake as the Romans simply reformed their line and attacked the lightly-armed and dismounted archers.

The Parthians were destroyed. Dio goes on to explain that the oblong, curved, and cylindrical shields were drawn up on the outside of the *testudo* whilst flat shields were raised above their heads. this was so strong that not only could men walk upon it but even horses and carriages. Thus a *testudo*, if held at an angle, could enable the rear rank to clamber over their comrades and attack from greater height. Vespasian's men must have been experts as each *oppidum* fell one after another. Many legionaries may have been present when each of the twenty *oppida* the sources describe fell.

Artillery

One of the reasons for Vespasian's success was Roman artillery, something that was probably unknown to many Britons. We recall Caesar's use of artillery from his warships to cover his legions as they waded ashore. They could provide a withering attack on exposed flanks. Unarmoured warriors, facing such weapons for the first time, would have been terrified.

One type of Roman artillery was the *ballista*. Early Roman *ballistae* used torsion-power with a twisted rope made from animal sinews to ratchet back a bowstring. Bolts or stones could be thrown several hundred metres when the ratchet was released. Those weapons could also be placed on towers attached to forts, siege towers or on ships. Lighter forms, *carroballistae,* were mounted on carts drawn by horses or mules.

Another type of Roman artillery was the *scorpio*, of which there were two main types. The first, a horizontal version, used torsion-power to shoot a bolt or stone. The second type, called an *onager*, consisted of a vertical arm which sprang forward to fire a rock or other missile. This could deliver a 25-kilo stone 440 metres. Archaeological finds of artillery stones in the north of Britain weigh up to 50 kilos. The effects of those weapons were gruesome and armour provided little to no protection.

In the fourth century, Vegetius described how each legion had ten *onagri*, one for each cohort, transported on ox-drawn wagons. A legion could march twenty miles in a day but oxen pulling a heavy carriage would be lucky to travel half that. Unsuited for battering down thick stone walls, it could break down less substantial structures and gates. As an anti-personnel weapon in a fixed position, it could create havoc and panic in an attacking force. It was very well suited to being a defensive weapon and we see this at the fort at Bremenium where the stone platforms measuring 7.5 by 10 metres were attached behind its walls.

Ammianus describes one example as follows:[11] Between two posts a long iron bar is fixed which projects out 'like a great ruler'. To this is attached a squared staff 'hollowed out along its length with a narrow groove'. In this groove the gunner places a long wooden arrow tipped with 'a great iron point'. The arrow, 'driven by the power within, flies from the ballista ... before the weapon is seen, the pain of a mortal wound makes itself felt.' He goes on to describe the scorpion or 'wild-ass'. A wooden arm, capable of holding a large stone, rises vertically (looking like a scorpion's sting) but can be pulled horizontally using iron hooks with tension supplied via the twisting of ropes. When released, the arm returns to the vertical with a violent kick (like an ass) and the wooden beam strikes a 'soft hair-cloth' cushion. Another name he gives is an 'onager'.

The Romans also used light artillery, and these could more easily be used on the battlefield. The ballista could fire stones or bolts of up to a foot in length, with one example from Spain estimated to have had a range of 300 metres.[12] Reproductions of a ballista and onager can be seen in figures 27 and 28. We can see examples of *carro-ballistae* on Trajan's column where the artillery is mounted on carts. Another example can be seen in figure 29 from the column of Marcus Aurelius. Similar artillery pieces would have been used by the Second.

Josephus was a first-century Romano-Jewish historian and military leader who initially fought against the Romans before surrendering

Figure 27: Reproduction of Roman Ballista. (Wikimedia commons)

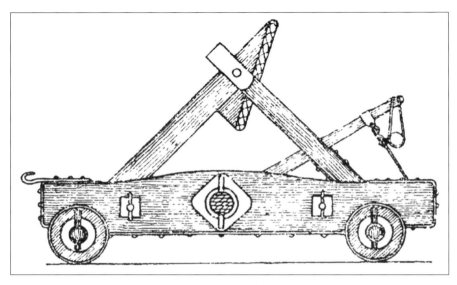

Figure 28: Drawing of a Roman onager. (Wikimedia commons)

Figure 29: Roman carroballista from column of Marcus Aurelius. (Wikimedia commons)

to Vespasian's army in 67 towards the end of Nero's reign. Josephus served as translator to Titus in the siege of Jerusalem in 70 (eventually taking the name Titus Flavius Josephus). He gives a vivid account of the effects of Roman artillery under Vespasian at the siege of Jotapata.[13]

The general set up 160 engines throwing stones, lances, arrows, darts and fire at the walls.

The Romans constructed a bank to reach the wall which caused the defenders to raise the height. The defenders attempted to protect themselves from missile attack by animal hides attached to poles. Still the 'darts and stones' kept up their deadly rain of fire, killing the defenders 'one upon another'. The force of the stones was so great that they 'hurt several at a time' and 'carried away the pinnacles of the wall, and broke off the corners of the towers'. Josephus himself was standing by a man near a wall when he was struck by a stone and 'his head was carried away... and his skull was flung as far as three furlongs'. This is nearly 2,000 feet or 670 yards, over a third of a mile. The noise of the stones and darts was tremendous. A pregnant woman was hit so violently the unborn child was ripped from her stomach and landed 300 feet away.

Procopius, writing in the sixth century, tells of *ballistae* that reach over 'two bow-shots'. Given Roman archers trained with targets set at about 180 metres we can estimate perhaps 400 metres. When it hits a tree or even a rock it pierces it easily.[14] Slings or 'wild-asses' were placed on the parapet walls of Rome to throw stones similar distances. The power of those weapons was described in vivid terms. At the siege of Rome in the sixth century, a large Gothic archer stood apart from his comrades shooting arrows up at the Roman defenders. A bolt was fired from a tower to his left, punched through his chest and embedded itself in a tree, leaving his corpse hanging.[15]

This demonstrates the destructive power of Roman artillery and, also, that Vespasian was well acquainted with the use of artillery. We can see how the Second Augusta might have gone about methodically preparing to assault a hillfort in Britain.

Roman forts

As Vespasian's army advanced westward, the supply fleet hugged the southern coast. Marching forts snaked across the countryside. Legionaries were well practised in the art of fort building. Rising at dawn they could march twenty miles in five hours using the 'military step' and twenty-four miles at 'full step'.[16] Work could then begin constructing a camp to protect them overnight. A good supply of water, firewood and fodder was important as was avoiding swampy areas and those overlooked by higher ground. Within as little as three hours the task would be complete.

The fourth-century writer Vegetius describes three types of camp:[17]

1. Where there's no immediate danger or for one night: A three-feet-deep fosse or ditch is cut five-feet wide with the turfs stacked up on the inside edge.
2. A 'stationary camp': a temporary fosse nine-feet wide and seven-feet deep.
3. When more serious forces threaten, a twelve- to seventeen-feet wide and nine-feet-deep fosse is built. Then inside an embankment four-feet high overlooks the fosse making it thirteen-feet deep.

Deep in hostile territory half of Vespasian's infantry and most of the cavalry would stand ready for an attack. The remaining troops would work on the ditch and embankment. The legionaries carried stakes to line the top of the embankment, but they probably provided a good temporary perimeter to prevent attacks by chariots and cavalry. Once complete, attackers faced a six-foot ditch behind which sat a six-foot-high bank, topped with a wooden palisade. Given time and resources, turrets and battlements could be constructed. Wide gates, protected by towers, were added, sometimes forty-feet wide, to allow rapid deployment against an attacking force.

Inside the wall a road, the *via sagularis*, ran around the perimeter of the camp allowing access to the ramparts from any part of the camp. This also reduced risk of damage from missile attack to the camp interior, especially from fire. Camp size obviously depended on the size of the force. Auxiliary camps along the Antonine Wall, for example, contained units of 500 and covered five acres. Legionary forts at York and Caerleon were ten times as large. Whatever the size, a visiting dignitary, or emperor, would be received, and perhaps stay in, the *praetorium* at the centre of the camp.

A more contemporary but anonymous Roman writer details slightly smaller dimensions compared to the later Vegetius:[18] A ditch, five-feet wide and three-feet deep surrounded a rampart nine-feet wide and six-feet in height. A second century source, *De Munitionibus Castrorum*, 'Concerning the fortifications of a military camp', gives a detailed description of the typical camp layout, generally a square or rectangular 'playing card' shape. This became common from the time of Claudius.

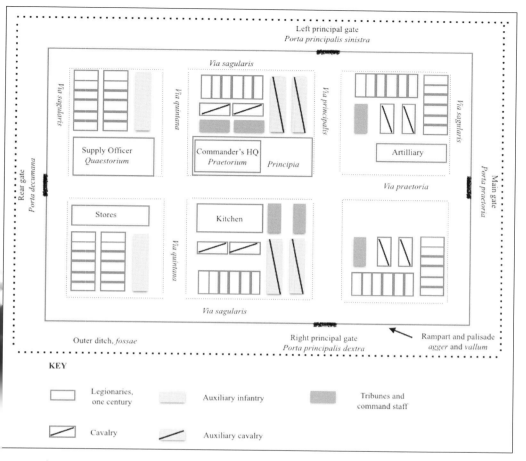

Figure 30: Typical Roman camp layout of legionary size.

Each side had a gate with two main roads connecting the gate opposite. These converged on the *principia*, at the centre of the camp. There lay the commander's headquarters and an open courtyard or forum with a raised platform to address the troops. Within the headquarters was the *aedes*, or shrine, where the legion or unit's standards were kept. Under this a strongroom was dug to hold the troops' coins. Also there were armouries, *armamentaria*, and even rooms for officer recreation, *scholae*. Established camps would have had baths, granaries and even shops with local settlements growing up around them. However, a marching camp in enemy territory would have no such luxuries.

Attached to the legions were a variety of specialists, *immunes*. Legionnaires with specific skills could also perform these vital functions; however, non-military personnel often accompanied the legions, adding considerably to the numbers. Larger and more established camps would have had a considerable number of such personnel. A list of some examples is instructive as to what a camp might have included:[19] surveyors, *mensores*; medical orderlies, *medici*; wound dressers, *capsarii*; veterinaries, *veterinarii*; master-builder, *architectus*; artillery makers/operators, *ballistrarii*; craftsmen, *fabri*; arrow-makers, *sagittarii*; bow-makers, *acuarii*; blacksmiths, *ferrarii*; bronze-smiths, *aerarii*; lead-makers, *plumbarii*; carpenters, *carpentarii*; sword-makers, *gladiatores*; hydraulic engineers, *aquilices*; stonemasons, *lapidarii*; hunters, *venatores*; armourers, *custodes armorum*; and millers, *polliones*. Specialist builders, shipwrights, ships' pilots, bridge-builders and artillery specialists were also present, as were priests to officiate at ceremonies and staff to look after sacrificial animals. Repair shops and manufacturers needed officers, managers and a sizeable workforce of skilled labourers. Clerks of various kinds were also needed for the granaries, general book-keeping; and for the deceased.

As Vespasian marched westwards some camps were dismantled the next morning, their ditches filled in to prevent use by the Britons. Others may have been garrisoned to guard any potential line of retreat. It is a little over 200 miles from Colchester to Exeter and less than 100 miles, following a coastal path, from any bases near the Solent, opposite the Isle of Wight, to Maiden Castle.

The Romans had no problem marching across the territory of the Durotriges, constructing camps as they went. What would have taken time was repeated long-drawn-out sieges. Unfortunately, we are left with no actual accounts of any battles or storming of *oppida*. If we take Suetonius at face value, Vespasian fought thirty battles and captured twenty towns. Whilst the Dobunni had surrendered early, it seems that at least two tribes put up a stout resistance.

The Britons

Before leaving Vespasian's victories in Britain, it is worth looking at the people living in the island he helped conquer. Indo-European languages originated in the lands around the Black Sea. Several branches, of which Celtic was one, spread west. It is not always simple to identify ethnicity or 'a people' through archaeology. Cultural practices change, evolve and are adopted from elsewhere. New practices in agriculture and farming appeared in c. 4,200-3,000 BC. A millennium and a half later saw the introduction of new skills of metalworking and an increase in trade. Several waves of immigration were accompanied by population growth and land clearance. As the late bronze age gave way to the iron age a unique culture developed, one with close links with northern and western Europe.

Language offers clues to cultural identity. A proto-Celtic language moved westwards into southern Europe after around 6,000 BC.[20] It had reached western Britain by c. 3,000 BC. In addition, the spread of 'Bell Beaker ideologies' accompanied a movement of peoples c. 2,700-2,400 BC. It is suggested that this movement of people in the mid-third millennium explains the difference between Goidelic (Q-Celtic) and Brythonic (P-Celtic), with the former dominating the west and north. The Britons against whom Caesar fought thus spoke a Brythonic, P-Celtic, language, similar to one found in Gaul.

Early Greek and Roman sources point to the Celtic people inhabiting the west, such as Narbonne in southern France and the Iberian peninsula. The same sources suggest that Britons shared a similar language and culture. Britain had experienced a 'descent into regionalism'.[21] Villages and 'open' settlements dominated in the east, with defended or enclosed homesteads in the west and north. The land was dotted with a patchwork of rival tribes with distinctive cultures and practices. Hillforts predominated in the south and parts of the west.

One of the earliest references to Britain comes from the Greek historian Herodotus in the fifth century BC. Known for its trade in tin, it received the name *Cassiterides*, 'tin islands'. A poem from the fourth century AD, *Ora maritima*, 'The Sea Coast', may have used an even earlier, sixth-century reference. This Greek navigational manual described two islands inhabited by two peoples, the Hierni and Albiones, these presumably being Ireland and Britain respectively.

The first eyewitness account occurred in c. 320 BC. The Greek explorer Pytheas travelled from Massalia to Armorica, circumnavigating Britain as he went. The book *On the Ocean* unfortunately did not survive but was referred to by later writers. Diodorus Siculus, in the first century BC, called the island *Pretanni*, thus the Britons would be the *Pretani* or

Priteni,'painted ones' or 'tattooed folk'. We recall Caesar's observation of the use of woad, a blue paint used in body decoration.

By the reign of Augustus, Strabo used the spelling *Pretannia* but Britannia was now a common alternative. Pliny the Elder, a contemporary of Vespasian, names the islands *Britannias* but the largest of them *Albion*. However, the survival of the P-sound may be heard in the later name *Picti*, for the northern tribes, and the Welsh name for Britain, *Prydain*. Certainly, by the second century AD, the B-spelling was dominant with Ptolemy referring to *Brettania*.

Strabo was a young man when Caesar invaded Britain. He gave a detailed description in *Geographica*.[22] The island was triangular in shape, lay opposite *Celtica*, Gaul, and was 4,300 *stadia* in length (a stadion is roughly 157 metres which equates to 675 kilometres or 420 miles). This is slightly longer than the actual distance from Kent to Land's End. Four main crossing points are listed: from the mouths of the Rhine and Seine facing Britain and the Loire and Garonne on the western Atlantic coast of Gaul.

Strabo continues: the island is flat although some regions are hilly and forested. Produce and exports include grain, cattle, gold, silver, iron, hides, slaves and hunting dogs. The last were especially highly prized and used in war. The men were taller than their Gallic cousins with a 'looser build' and 'not so yellow-haired'. Slave boys seen in Rome were 'half a foot above the tallest people in the city'. Culturally and socially, they were described as similar to Gauls but were 'simpler and more barbaric'.

He goes on to describe their settlements: placed in forests and fenced by felled trees forming spacious circular enclosures within which huts and cattle can be found. The weather is 'more rainy than snowy; and on the days of clear sky fog prevails so long a time that throughout a whole day the sun is to be seen for only three or four hours round about midday'.

Much of Strabo's account we can take with a large pinch of salt and put down to Roman propaganda. In his description of Ireland, the inhabitants are even more savage than the Britons: cannibals who 'openly have intercourse, not only with the other women, but also with their mothers and sisters'.

Caesar is perhaps more reliable.[23] Unlike Strabo, who claimed the Britons had no agriculture (despite mentioning grain), Caesar describes a rich agricultural tradition similar to Gaul with 'farm-buildings very close together', and a 'great store of cattle'. Coastal tribes, such as the Atrebates and Belgae, were believed to have migrated from Gaul. The south-eastern tribes, such as the Canti, were apparently more civilised. Whilst those in the interior 'do not sow corn, but live on milk and flesh' he doesn't claim they are unclothed as other Roman writers do. Instead, they wear skins.

It is possible he misunderstood cultural traditions but, as with later writers, he claimed they held a communal type of lifestyle with households of ten or twelve men, often related. They held their wives and children in common, a point alluded to in the early third century by Cassius Dio. The climate is described as more temperate than in Gaul with winter 'more moderate'. The people 'dye themselves with woad, which produces a blue colour, and makes their appearance in battle more terrible. They wear long hair, and shave every part of the body save the head and the upper lip.'

A little over a century after Mons Graupius, Cassius Dio gives an interesting perspective on Britons during the Caledonian campaign of Septimius Severus in 208-11. The main tribes the Romans fought against were the Caledonians and the Maeatae. It is thought various tribes had come together, merging into two confederations. The Maeatae were located in central Scotland and the Caledonians were said to live further north.

These Britons had no cities or walls and lived in the 'wild and waterless mountains and desolate and swampy plains'. He claimed that they did not farm but lived on wild game and fruits. All this could be Roman propaganda but, according to Dio, the Britons lived in tents, and wore no clothes or shoes. Given the climate and occasional successful recorded raids we must doubt these accounts. Dio continues that the Britons had a love of plunder and chose their bravest and boldest to lead them. They used chariots and 'swift horses' and, unlike at Mons Graupius, the infantry were 'very firm in standing their ground'.

They were armed with shields, daggers and short spears, the latter of which had a 'bronze apple' at one end to bash against their shields to terrify their enemies. They had a reputation for enduring extremes of hunger and cold, plunging into swamps and living there for days 'with only their heads above water'. Whatever the truth, the northern Britons avoided pitched battles and used guerrilla tactics. Sheep and cattle were used as bait to lure the Romans into ambushes. Severus is said to have lost 50,000 men in the campaign. This implies a certain level of sophistication in enemy tactics and ability.

Eventually the Britons were forced to come to terms, at which point we get a fascinating snapshot into the cultural and social life. Again, we read they were said to 'possess their women and children in common'. During negotiations between the emperor and a chieftain of the Caledonians, Argentocoxus, the empress Julia Augusta entertained the Caledonian's wife. The empress joked about the 'free intercourse' the women of Britain had with their men. Cassius Dio seems rather impressed with the reply: 'We fulfil the demands of nature in a much better way than do you Roman women; for we consort openly with the best men, whereas you let yourselves be debauched in secret by the vilest.'

Herodian in the early third century described the Britons as 'savage and warlike' and 'strangers to clothing', wearing 'ornaments of iron' around their waists and necks. Their bodies were tattooed with coloured designs and pictures of animals. Armed with a spear, narrow shield and a sword suspended from a belt hanging 'from their otherwise naked bodies', they wore no helmets or breastplates which must have put them at a disadvantage in combat against the heavily-armed legionaries. The Romans won 'frequent battles and skirmishes', but the Britons slipped away easily, using their knowledge of the woods and marshes.

Tacitus wrote a little after Vespasian's reign and provides contemporary, and perhaps more accurate, information.[24] The soil is fertile and the weather rainy and cloudy though the temperature is moderate. The tribes of the south-east are similar to the Gauls in language and culture, sharing some of their sacred rites and superstitions. Some differences are noted: The Silures of southern Wales have a swarthy complexion and curled hair whilst the Caledonians are large-limbed and red-haired with a Germanic origin.

The Britons generally are described as more ferocious in war than their Gallic cousins, although they had been softened by peace. We then get some important information concerning military matters: their strength lay in their infantry whilst some tribes use chariots, the 'most honourable person guides the reins', while others fight from the platform. Their weakness lay in their disunity and tendency for civil war allowing the Romans to divide and conquer.

Tacitus goes on to describe how the Romans won the hearts and minds of the conquered. The Britons submitted to levies and tributes 'if they are not treated injuriously'. They provided a Roman education for the sons of British chieftains. Warriors who had previously 'disdained to make use of the Roman language, were now ambitious of becoming eloquent'. Roman habits began to be emulated and 'held in honour'. Britons took to wearing the toga. Slowly the elites were seduced by Roman baths and fine dining.

Economic growth, towns, trade links and taxes wove a web of Roman civilisation that brought about their own enslavement.

A battle scenario

We can only speculate on how Vespasian's advance westward progressed. Given the battles at Watling Street and Mons Graupius, there is no reason to suspect the Britons fared any better against the Second Augusta. There's no record of a pitched battle and it is likely the Britons resorted to guerrilla tactics before sheltering within their hillforts.

The images in figures 31-37 provide a good portrayal of Roman and British warriors. Let us imagine that the Britons felt confident enough to attempt to halt Vespasian's march. The Britons would have seen them

Figure 31: Legionary legate and legionaries of the Second Legion. (Alisa Vanlint of Legio Secunda Augusta and Ludus Augusta)

Figure 32: Legionary wearing *lorica* hamata. (Alisa Vanlint of Legio Secunda Augusta and Ludus Augusta)

stop in late afternoon to make camp. They would have noticed how formidable the defences looked. With artillery and siege equipment, any attacks would prove costly. Every morning the Romans would break camp and march out in good order. Perhaps the best time to attack was mid-morning after several hours' march but before they stopped to make camp. Strung out as Varus had been in the Teutoburg Forest, they could be vulnerable.

Yet a well-trained force, with experienced scouts, could respond to such threats quickly. Forming up into two rows of five cohorts each, the

Figure 33: A Briton despatching a Roman soldier. (Alisa Vanlint of Legio Secunda Augusta and Ludus Augusta)

Figure 34: Battle re-enactment. (Zane Green of Legio Secunda Augusta)

Figure 35: Battle re-enactment. (Zane Green of Legio Secunda Augusta)

Figure 36: Britons. (Zane Green of Legio Secunda Augusta)

Figure 37: Britons
(Zane Green of Legio
Secunda Augusta)

Romans would deploy the auxiliary troops to the front and sides with cavalry to the flanks. Vespasian would watch impassively as thousands of Britons massed. Chariots and swift horses would wheel back and forth delivering javelins. Those would have little effect on the well-armoured front ranks. Shields, covered in leather, offered excellent protection. The Romans' own cavalry and missile troops would drive them off. Eventually, the Britons would have to decide to charge or retreat.

The fourth-century writer Vegetius stated that the Romans trained to fire their bows at targets placed 200 yards away. A third of the legionaries might be deployed temporarily as archers. Slingshots could also prove deadly. The Britons would have to decide fast. If the Romans had time to deploy their scorpions and ballistae they would be sitting targets. Even at 200 yards arrows could prove fatal to unarmoured warriors. The majority of warriors would be carrying a spear and shield, making it difficult to sprint the full distance over rough ground. But at 150 yards the arrows start to become accurate and by 50 yards they are deadly.[25]

However, that may not have been enough to break the massed formation bearing down on the Romans. The auxiliaries would discharge their weapons and retreat to the flanks. Now the Britons faced a wall of shields. The first five cohorts numbered over 2,600 men. Standing six ranks deep, they would stretch over 400 metres. At three ranks they would cover half a mile, backed up by the remaining five cohorts. At 30 yards 5,000 iron-tipped *pila* rained down from the front ranks, followed shortly after by a further 5,000. Shorter spears or javelins had an effective range of around 12–15 metres.[26]

By the time the Britons reached the front ranks of their enemies their own front ranks would have been decimated. The dead and injured would litter the ground and break up the advance as well as crucially hindering any retreat. Shields, rendered useless by *pila*, would be tossed aside. The Britons now had to break through. Yet every spear and sword thrust seemed to hit wood or metal. Even those that got past the shield seemed to slide off the curved surfaces of helmets or armour. In contrast, the deadly gladius stabbed out into bare flesh or cut through into leather. Unhelmeted warriors were highly susceptible to head blows. All the time *pila*, javelins, slings and arrows fell upon the rear ranks.

The Britons would have relied much on this initial charge to break the Romans' formation. Failure would result in the front ranks becoming exhausted, unable to go forward but pushed on from behind. The Romans simply had to hold their ground. Timing was everything. A sudden flank or rear attack could be enough. Or perhaps on a signal the front ranks advanced slowly, step by step. The Britons edged back. Some tripped over fallen comrades. A steady retreat turned to panic. Faced with an impenetrable wall of death moving towards them, one they couldn't break through, the Britons started to break.

Once an army breaks, it is at its most vulnerable. With backs to their foes, the soldiers are easily chased down by pursuing cavalry. Any injured left on the battlefield are easily despatched. Given the lack of any references to largescale battles, it is likely this scenario played out on a small scale several times. Perhaps a single auxiliary unit of 500 was caught in an attempted ambush. It's even possible that the Britons may have won on occasion. But the relentless advance of the Romans was unstoppable. The Britons were forced to hide behind their earthworks and ditches, then watch their hillforts fall one after another.

How could Vespasian capture such a large number so quickly? Surrounding a settlement with artillery is a fairly quick process but how long would it take to construct a ramp? Maiden Castle rises 40 metres above the surrounding countryside and the surrounding rings of banks and ditches cover a width of 120 metres. Ignoring the banks (which would lessen the time) one could make a quick calculation for the length of a ramp: 126 metres. If the ramp is a generous 10 metres wide this gives a volume of 24,000 cubic metres. The British Army calculates one man can move 0.3 cubic metre of earth in one hour, half the amount in chalk or rocky ground.[27]

This equates to 80,000-man hours. Space would be restricted, so it might be practical to have a single cohort working on the ramp behind screens. They could even work round the clock by firelight with cohorts being relieved every few hours. Such a construction could be completed in a week.

Soldiers under Titus constructed a seven-kilometre siege wall in just three days when besieging Jerusalem in 70. At Masada they built a 225-metre-long ramp to reach a height of 75 metres from which a siege engine was able to punch a hole through the defences. At the siege of Alesia in 52 BC, Caesar's men built ten miles of fortifications surrounding Vercingetorix and 80,000 Gauls in the hillfort. This took only three weeks. A subsequent outer ring, 14 miles long, was constructed to prevent a relief force breaking through.

Figure 38: Roman siege ramp at Masada. (Wikimedia Commons)

It is thus possible to estimate how long it would take to capture twenty hillforts. Vespasian's siege at Jotapata during the Judean campaign lasted forty-seven days. But that was an exceptionally difficult nut to crack. Caesar's siege of Alesia lasted approximately two weeks. If we estimate a similar timeframe, or less, for Vespasian's objectives then it is just possible that he might have achieved this in a single year. Especially if he split his force and some objectives were relatively small. What is certain is that the numbers are no exaggeration given Vespasian's time in Britain.

Summary

Within four years of the fall of Camulodunum, Plautius had secured much of southern and central Britain. Vespasian had reached as far west as modern Exeter. The Durotriges, Dumnonii and other tribes were subdued after much hard fighting. The new province, *Britannia*, extended to a border marked by the Fosse Way, linking Exeter in the southwest to Lincoln in the east. After the year 47 expansion continued. The Fourteenth Legion advanced into the Midlands, first based at Manduessedum, Mancetter and then Viroconium, Wroxeter. The Ninth marched north to Lindum, Lincoln, whilst the Twentieth remained at Camulodunum. Later it was to move west to Gloucester to support the advance into Wales.

Vespasian returned to Rome. His career would take a number of twists and turns on his way to glory. First, he had to survive the chaotic reign of Nero and the often-fatal palace intrigues of the elites. Finally, he found himself one of four claimants for the throne in one of the most tumultuous years of Roman history. All that was in the future. In 47 Vespasian was aboard a ship heading for northern Gaul and a return to Rome. He had proven himself an able general and gained a reputation that would stand him in good stead.

Chapter 5

THE FALL AND RISE OF VESPASIAN'S CAREER

W ith much of southern Britain secure by the end of the year 47, Vespasian was sent back to Rome. Once there, he received the *ornamenta* and two priesthoods for his exploits. In 51 he finally obtained the coveted consulship. This was a great achievement for a former equestrian and would have been the pinnacle of a proud career. Had someone suggested at this point the Judo-Claudian line would fall, and Vespasian might aspire to an even greater office, they would have been laughed out of the Senate. At best, he hoped the consulship might open doors to a lucrative governorship of a proconsul province. Legally, Vespasian had to wait five years before being eligible for such a post. However, the downfall of Massalina, Claudius's third wife, was to prove a pivotal point in Vespasian's career.

In early 49 Claudius married a final time, to his niece Agrippina, the sister of Caligula. The consulship of 51 was to be Vespasian's last high-profile appointment under Claudius. He found himself slowly falling out of favour. He wasn't alone. The freedman Narcissus had been one of the emperor's most trusted men. He sat on the *Consilium Principis* and was helpful in Vespasian's career. It was Narcissus who had obtained him command of the Second Augusta in Germania. This was the same Narcissus who shamed the reluctant legionaries to board ship in the invasion of 43.

With Vespasian frozen out, Narcissus hung on in an increasingly fractious palace. Just three years after Vespasian's consulship, and seemingly the highpoint of his career, the reign of Claudius ended. It was October 54 and this most unlikely of emperors was 63 years old when he fell ill and died. Suetonius tells us that 'it is commonly agreed that Claudius was killed by poison'. Whilst the method was debated, all eyes looked to Agrippina.

Her son, Nero, had been adopted by Claudius. Nero was four years older than Britannicus, Claudius's son by the disgraced Massalina. But Britannicus was fast approaching manhood and rumours were that Claudius regretted both his marriage to Agrippina and the adoption of Nero. Agrippina had to move fast. A dish of mushrooms allegedly provided the means, possibly followed by more of the deadly potion added to the emperor's porridge. With Claudius dead, Nero was in position and a cull of Claudius's supporters began. Narcissus was forced to suicide.

The immediate threat to Nero was Britannicus. Within four months he, too, would meet the same fate as his father. He died a day before his fourteenth birthday, when he was due to be presented with the *toga virilis*. All fingers once more pointed to Agrippina and Nero with poison again the *modus operandi*. Not only was Vespasian seen as friendly to Narcissus but his son, Titus, was a childhood friend of Britannicus. In fact, he was said to have been sitting next to the poor boy when he died and had even become ill himself after drinking from the same cup.

When Claudius died in October 54 Nero, two months short of his sixteenth birthday, had been the natural choice to succeed, but it was no secret who the power behind the throne was. Agrippina brought in her own supporters and Vespasian was frozen out. Suetonius states that he passed the next years in virtual retirement, fearing Agrippina's influence, and her deep loathing for anyone connected to Narcissus.

If this situation had continued long enough Vespasian may never had the chance for the throne. Indeed, Nero's reign might have been very different. But the new emperor chafed at his mother's control.

Sources differ as to how Agrippina died but they seem to concur that, five years into his reign, Nero had become frustrated by his mother's overbearing influence. First, he tried to poison her and when that failed a false ceiling was constructed to fall upon her while she slept. Yet that just resulted in another failure. He designed a ship that would fall apart in mid-water in the hope it would look as if she had drowned in an accident. But Agrippina proved a strong swimmer and made it to shore.

Tacitus tells us that three assassins finished the job whilst Suetonius claims Nero faked an assassination attempt and implicated his mother, resulting in her execution. Cassius Dio has just one assassin completing the task but embellishes the act with Agrippina's last words. Recognising the man sent and guessing his purpose, she leapt from her bed and ripped open her clothing. Pointing to her womb she cried: 'Strike here, Anicetus, strike here, for this bore Nero.'[1]

Agrippina died in March 59 and it is perhaps telling that Vespasian was back in favour, obtaining the proconsulship of Africa by the year 62. Vespasian's rule in the province was not universally popular and at one point he was pelted with turnips at the port of Hadrumetum. However, Suetonius claims the new governor ruled with integrity and honour. Unlike other governors, Vespasian did not use the position to enrich himself. In fact, he used so much of his own money and resources that he allegedly went into a business trading in mules, a fact his detractors later used against him, nicknaming Vespasian 'the muleteer'.

Despite rumours of the murders of Claudius and Brittanicus, the early years of Nero's reign were considered a time of stability and good governance. He had been tutored by Seneca who, together with Burrus, guided the young emperor. In his early reign he had actually entertained progressive inclinations:[2] He tried to abolish indirect taxes, stop the killing of gladiators and criminals in public spectacles and restrict capital punishment. The turning point appears to have been around the year 62, after which he became more despotic and murderous.

He divorced Octavia, daughter of his adoptive father, the former emperor Claudius, and later had her executed and the head presented to his new wife Poppaea. Within three years Poppaea had followed her rival, reportedly kicked to death by Nero in a temper. She was pregnant with their second child, the first having died as an infant two years previously. A serious plot in c. 65 resulted in a series of executions, banishments and forced suicides. Punishments continued over the next three years which served only to undermine any support and goodwill Nero had had in his earlier years.

It was into this increasingly unstable court that Vespasian returned sometime in the early 60s after his proconsulship in Africa. Titus had served with distinction in Germania and Britannia and was also back in Rome. Though back in Nero's good graces, Vespasian made a near-fatal mistake whilst travelling with the emperor's entourage through Greece. During one of many musical performances, Vespasian had the habit of leaving early or falling asleep. He did it once too often and fell 'into the deepest disfavour' and was banished from court. Vespasian retired again, this time to a small out of the way town and awaited his fate. This could easily have been the end of Vespasian's career, or even his life, in which case he would have remained a mere footnote in Roman history.

Events, however, were to turn back in his favour again. A serious revolt in the east presented Nero with a problem. A legionary commander was killed, and the governor of Syria's army routed. He turned to a trusted commander but one who, 'being of a modest name and family offered no risk'. Vespasian was back in favour and heading for Judea. He took his 27-year-old son Titus with him.

The Jewish War

Judea had come under Roman influence when Pompey campaigned in the east in 63 BC. By 37 BC Herod the Great was seen as a Roman client king. In AD 6 it became a Roman province ruled by equestrian prefects appointed by the emperor, one of the few provinces not administered by someone of senatorial rank.

A number of problems came to a head which sparked what became known as 'The First Jewish War'. The imposition of an alien Emperor cult was just one. There were also economic concerns, with debt and land shortage being major contributors. In addition, an element of class hatred was compounded by a split between town dwellers and those in the countryside. Much of the ruling class were seen to be in cahoots with the Roman governors, many of whom had treated the general population with contempt.

In 66 Nero commanded the equestrian governor of Judea, Gessius Florus, to confiscate money from the Temple treasury in Jerusalem. There was significant resistance. More humiliating for the new governor were the mocking jokes about passing the hat around for 'that poor procurator Florus'. Florus was no master diplomat. The governor's heavyhanded response did little to de-escalate the situation. Innocents were arrested and crucified. Attempts by the high priest, Ananias, and the Jewish prince Marcus Julius Agrippa to calm the situation simply convinced many Jews that their leaders were corrupt.

An added religious element was a widespread belief in a prophecy from the *Book of Numbers* suggesting that a comet would herald the coming of a Messiah. Suetonius notes 'an old and established belief widespread throughout the East, it was fated that at that time men coming from Judea would take control of the world.' The appearance of a comet in 64 had many believing their deliverance from the Romans was at hand. Religious tensions were already heightened by perceived insults, such as sacrificing to Roman gods outside a synagogue and building works impinging on a synagogue in the capital. The raiding of the palace treasury and brutal punishments by Florus lit the touch-paper.

The subsequent unrest resulted in the governor fleeing the city and the remaining Roman garrison came under siege within the walls. Elsewhere, the Roman guards at Masada were massacred and the stronghold was occupied by the rebels, led by Menahem ben Judah. Those rebels were called *Sicarians*, 'dagger men', and after their victory they headed for Jerusalem. Once there, they executed the high priest Ananias and any moderates were killed or driven out. Menahem would eventually be killed by a rival zealot, Eleazar, and the *Sicarians* retreated back to Massada where they held out to the end of the bitter war. As fighting broke out in the city between factions of the rebels, Rome's client king, Herod, fled Jerusalem. He was closely followed by the troops of Rome's other client king in the region, Agrippa.

The Roman guards in Herod's palace were alone and besieged. They were eventually forced to surrender after assurances of safe passage. The promises proved false, and they were butchered. An orgy of bloodletting ensued across Judea. A similar massacre was carried out against the Jews in Caesarea by the Greek inhabitants over fifty miles north-west of Jerusalem. The Jews in turn drove out Greek inhabitants and Roman garrisons across Judea, Galilee and the Golan heights.

Wholesale unrest spread across the province. Cestius Gallus, governor of Syria, set out with over 11,000 legionaries and 5,000 auxiliary troops. Client kings such as Agrippa II, who ruled the region around Galilee, supplied a further 14,000, a third of them cavalry. A force of 30,000 should have proved effective. As they advanced, Roman garrisons further south continued to fall, such as Jericho and Machaerus. At Jericho the entire Roman garrison was wiped out.

Gallus's army replied with brutality, carrying out their own massacres at Jaffa and Caesarea. Finally, the Romans reached Jerusalem, now swollen with refugees. The siege proved ineffective, and Gallus began a retreat to the coast. This proved to be a disastrous decision. En route his army was ambushed. The Battle of Beth Horon was a humiliating defeat for the Romans, who lost 6,000 men and an *aquila*, the legion's eagle, to a Jewish army led by Eleazar.

In Jerusalem a Judean provisional government was formed by the rebels. Meanwhile, Nero replaced Florus with Antonius Julianus as governor of Judea. Crucially, he appointed Vespasian as *legatus Augusti pro praetore exercitus Iudaici*, the Propraetorian Legate of the Army of Judea. That was a pivotal moment in Vespasian's career and, indeed, history. Without the Jewish revolt, Florus's heavy-handedness or the defeat at Beth Horon, Vespasian would not have been in position at the crucial moment, the year before he took the throne.

Vespasian travelled across the Hellespont and down into Syria via the Cilician gates, arriving in Antioch by 1 March 67. There he took command of two legions, X Fretensis and V Macedonica and received the support of various client kings. He was joined by his son, Titus, coming up from Alexandria with Legio XV Apollinaris. His forces were considerable, greater even than Plautius had at his disposal for the conquest of Britain, twenty-three auxiliary units, ten of which were *milliariae*, numbering over 16,000 men. Together with the three legions and client kings, he had around 50,000 troops.[3]

Beginning in 67 Vespasian directed his first efforts at securing the coastal strip and the conquest of Galilee. The Romans reached the stronghold of Jotapata in late May and began a bloody siege. By 68 Vespasian's troops had secured Galilee and the Jordan Valley and driven the enemy from the Golan heights.

Titus Flavius Josephus, the Jewish military leader and historian, fought against Vespasian's army in this First Jewish War. He was captured after the siege at Jotapata. His most influential work, *Bellum Judaicum*, 'The Jewish War', provides the best contemporary account of the conflict. When Jotapata fell, the Romans massacred thousands. Josephus had been trapped with forty of his comrades, all but two of whom committed suicide. Brought before Vespasian, he declared that a prophecy had convinced him that Vespasian would be emperor. That was enough to save him, and he eventually gained his freedom and Roman citizenship, serving the Flavians.

Josephus admired the Roman organisation, and it is through his account that we get one of the best contemporary records of Roman history. He noted that the legionaries exercised every day 'with great diligence, as if it were in time of war'. So realistic were the training exercises that one would not be mistaken in describing 'their exercises as un-bloody battles, and their battles bloody exercises'. The training was combined with a strict discipline which instilled both fear and obedience. Capital punishment was not only for running away, but for 'slothfulness and inactivity'. But it was their camps that Josephus seemed most impressed with.

Josephus describes in great detail how, after a day's march, the Romans would not fight until they walled in their camp with a palisade and towers. Artillery was placed to fire arrows, darts and stones. Four large gates, one on each side, allowed rapid deployment. The camp was divided into streets with the commander's tent in the centre. The trench, Josephus estimated, was four cubits in depth and length. A cubit was a measurement from the elbow to tips of the fingers, roughly 18 inches or 45 cm. Thus, roughly the height of a man in depth and width, with the bank rising by the same amount behind the fosse. The times for sleeping, watching, eating and rising were all signalled by trumpets. When the camp was vacated the whole process was again signalled by the sound of trumpets, from the tents being dismantled to the camp being levelled and burned.

The soldiers marched out as though ready for war. In the vanguard were lightly-armed auxiliary troops and archers, followed by heavy Roman infantry and cavalry. Next came the camp builders, ten men from each century, with their tools. Behind them came the baggage train of the senior officers, followed by the general himself and his personal bodyguard. Then came the legionary cavalry and mules with the siege equipment. The officers, legionary legates and tribunes and the auxiliary prefects accompanied the eagles, standards and trumpeters. Behind them marched the bulk of the legionaries, six abreast, followed by the servants and baggage with auxiliary and allied troops. A rearguard of light and heavy infantry and cavalry completed the spectacle.

At the beginning of the campaign, a Jewish attack at Ascalon had been beaten off with heavy losses for the besiegers. Vespasian then marched from Antioch to Ptolemais. A relief force was sent to Sepphoris and a Jewish attack led by Josephus was repelled. Titus came from Achaia to Alexandria and from there took the Fifteenth Legion to Ptolemais to join up with his father's two legions, the Fifth and Tenth. They began to cut a bloody swath through Galilee. The population fled to the walled towns and cities, the largest of which was Jotapata.

Vespasian came first to Gadara and took it quickly. He slew all the youth with 'no mercy on any age', sold some into slavery and burned the city. Many towns in the region earned the same fate before he turned towards Jotapata where Josephus and the other commanders prepared for the assault. Vespasian arrived at the northern side of the city and pitched tent on a hill seven furlongs, (just under a mile) from the city. Next day, the Romans attacked but were beaten off in the open ground before the gates. By then the city had been surrounded with no way out. For five days there was bitter fighting beneath the city walls as the Jews sallied out time and time again.

Jotapata was built on a precipice, surrounded on three sides by deep valleys and mountains. Only on the north side could an attack be made. Vespasian decided that a long siege was inevitable and ordered a bank to be constructed up to the walls. A huge quantity of stones and trees were ripped from the mountainsides as engineers got to work. Screens and 'hurdles' were put in place to protect them as the defenders hurled everything they could at them.

Vespasian, in turn, placed 160 siege engines to throw iron, stone and fire at the walls. Some of the stones weighed a talent, a unit of weight approximately 25 kilograms or 57 pounds. The defenders tried to destroy those with artillery of their own or sallied out in raiding parties. As the bank inched closer to the wall, Josephus ordered the battlements raised and extra towers built. Ingeniously, he contrived a screen made from ox-hides to protect the workmen from artillery fire.

This stratagem and repeated sallies sapped the strength of the Romans. Denied a quick victory, the frustrated Vespasian decided his best course was to starve the enemy out. However, the siege dragged on, and the Jewish sallies continued. The Romans resolved to bring up a huge battering ram. The Jews responded with bitumen, pitch and brimstone and set fire to the engine and hurdles: 'what cost the Romans a great deal of pains, was in one hour consumed.' Still, the Romans persevered. The engine was repaired and another attack launched.

It was then that a Jewish defender called Eleazar dramatically stood up on the wall holding 'a great stone'. He threw it down upon the ram. His aim was good, and the head broke off the siege engine. Jumping down from the walls, Eleazar carried off the trophy and held it aloft, despite being wounded by five Roman 'darts'. The Jews sallied out again and drove off the Fifth and Tenth Legions, burning many engines as they did so.

The Jews were initially jubilant but the Romans rebuilt their ram and were soon at the wall again. It was at this point that Vespasian was struck by an arrow in his foot. There was a brief pause as his worried commanders rushed to his tent. But their commander was made of stern stuff, and re-assured the men, rallied his troops and the assault continued.

Josephus described the terrible noise and effects of the siege engines with scores of ballistae and onagers firing stone and iron. The sound of those striking stone and brick must have been tremendous, interspersed with the sound of splintering wood as the great stones crashed into buildings within the city walls. Perhaps worse was the unmistakeable dull thud when missiles hit flesh. A man standing close to Josephus was decapitated by a stone and his head flung three furlongs (about 600 metres). In another horrific anecdote, a pregnant woman was struck and her unborn infant ripped from her belly and flung half a furlong (about 100 metres).

At one point in the siege a section of wall appears to have been breached. The Romans attacked. Infantry advanced in *testudo* formation against the damaged section, supported by archers and slingers. The Jews replied with burning oil. The Romans were beaten off again, this time with heavy losses. Only six defenders were killed, although Josephus tells us 300 were injured.

Vespasian ordered the bank to be raised higher and three towers constructed, protected by iron plates. These proved devastating for those defending the wall. The Jews had no choice but to sally out in an attempt to destroy them. Meanwhile, Vespasian sent his general Trajan, and then his son Titus, to capture the nearby city of Japha. The city fell and the Romans let loose their frustrations on the poor citizens. As many as 15,000 Jews were slaughtered with the survivors (just 2,150) taken into slavery. A further 11,600 were killed at a nearby mountain called *Gerizzim*.

Back at Jotapata, the siege dragged on day after bloody day. In the end it was not Roman siege technology that broke the deadlock. A deserter betrayed the rebels and informed Vespasian of the best time and place to attack. Titus, having returned, led a small band of the Fifteenth Legion to reach a section of the wall. They slit the throats of the sleeping guards and entered the city. It was the forty-seventh day of the siege. The Jews awoke to the horror of their situation.

The killing began. Josephus estimated 40,000 were slaughtered. Remembering the hardships of the siege, the burning oil and their dead comrades, the Romans showed no mercy. Vespasian was similarly disposed. He ordered the city demolished and the remains burned.

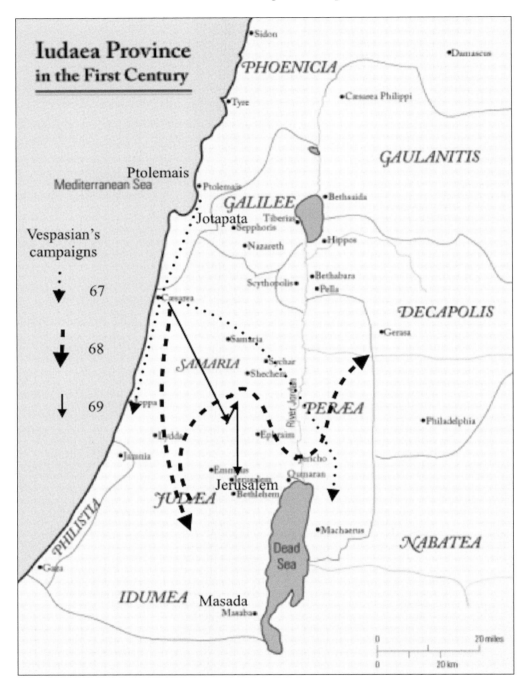

Figure 39: Map of Vespasian's campaign in Judea. (Wikimedia Commons)

Inside, the Jewish commanders began committing suicide. Fortuitously for Josephus he was one of the last two alive when the Romans captured him. Dragged to the general, he claimed a divine revelation had told him Vespasian would be emperor. If Vespasian was suspicious of his captive's motives, within a couple of years the prediction would come true. Later, Josephus was sent with Titus to negotiate the surrender of Jerusalem. Jotapata fell around 2 July 67. By the end of that year the revolt in the north had largely been crushed. Towns across the region were re-taken: Afeq, Lydda, Javneh, and Jaffa.

The following year was one of the most remarkable in Roman history. Vespasian was preparing his attack on Jerusalem when a messenger brought the most astounding news. The emperor was dead. Killed by his own hand as his power disintegrated after a revolt that had begun in Gaul. A new emperor had already been proclaimed by the senate. Titus was sent to Rome to congratulate the new emperor, Galba, and receive confirmation of their position or receive new orders. Just a few months later, news of Galba's death caused Vespasian to halt operations altogether. Two new emperors now faced each other. Otho had Rome and the senate. Vitellius had the legions of the Rhine.

Important decisions were made all across the empire. Picking the right side early might lead to plum jobs, riches and political survival. Pick the wrong side and it could mean disgrace, loss of position or even death. But, perhaps for the first time Vespasian, the equestrian from the Sabine country, began to ponder his own chances. The man who had virtually retired into obscurity during Nero's early reign found himself in command of several battle-hardened legions just as Rome seemed to be tearing itself apart.

The Contenders

Before we turn to the outbreak of civil war, it would be helpful to take a brief look at the contenders. However, first we will take a brief look at the incumbent, Nero. We can see a representative in the figure below. Suetonius described him as of average height, blond hair and blue eyes. A thick neck, thin legs and prominent belly. His features 'regular rather than attractive'. His body was marked with spots and he had an unpleasant smell. Yet his health was good, and he was 'shameless' in appearance

Figure 40: Bust of Nero. (Wikimedia Commons)

and dress, putting his hair in rows of curls and greeting guests barefoot in an unbelted silk dressing-gown. He had a love of all the arts: poetry, painting, sculpture and music. He was also a keen wrestler and fan of chariot racing. His greatest love was perhaps singing but Suetonius states his main driving force was to be popular. None of this was of any help to him when the legates began to march.

Servius Sulpicius Galba hailed from a great family of patrician rank with a long illustrious pedigree. Born on 24 December, 3 BC he had risen to be a consul by the year AD 33, after serving as imperial governor of Aquitania. He added governorships of Upper Germany and Africa, the latter in the year 45. The first four emperors, from Augustus to Claudius, all thought very highly of him.

In his forties or fifties, he had lost his wife, Lepida, and two children during the reign of Claudius but unusually had refused to re-marry, remaining single for the rest of his life. When Nero came to power, like Vespasian, he slid into semi-retirement. However, around the year 60 he was appointed governor of Hispanic Terraconensis. Eight years later he was still there as Nero's reign began to crumble. He was 70 years old.

Suetonius described him as of medium height, bald with blue eyes and a hooked nose. A heavy eater, on his right side his flesh hung down so much it could hardly be kept in place by a bandage. He was so crippled by arthritis that he could not wear shoes for long periods or even unroll parchments or hold books.

He had a reputation of being strict, prohibiting the practice of buying leave, and improved training for veterans and new recruits alike. When Caligula visited the provinces, Galba's troops gave the most favourable impression. Galba, then in his forties, had run alongside the emperor's chariot, shield in hand, for twenty miles. He had also displayed loyalty in the past. When Caligula was assassinated, he dismissed advice to take advantage of the situation and supported Claudius, an act that endeared him to the new emperor.

In Spain his reputation for strictness and cruelty continued. A money-changer, convicted of fraud, had his hands cut of and nailed to his counting-table. A guardian who had poisoned his charge was crucified, a punishment usually reserved for non-Romans. When the man complained that he was, in fact, a citizen Galba's only 'concession' was to have the cross raised slightly and painted white. In his final governorship in Spain, he ruled in 'a changeable and inconsistent manner' and 'sank into sloth and idleness'. Such was the man who found himself in position to seize ultimate power. Elderly and arthritic. Cruel and avaricious. Strict, but inconsistent with his previous self-discipline seemingly gone.

Our second contender was the much younger Marcus Salvius Otho, born on 28 April 32. Like Vespasian's, his family had originally been of equestrian rank, although they had risen to patrician status under Augustus. His father, Lucius Otho, was said to have so closely resembled the Emperor Tiberius that some gossiped he was his son.

In childhood he had been 'extravagant and wild', earning him regular beatings from his father. As a young man he enjoyed the nightlife and fashionable pursuits Rome had to offer. He was said to have wandered the streets at night attacking the drunk or vulnerable. He managed to become one of Nero's most intimate friends and they shared similar interests 'since they were alike in character'. Some alleged they were lovers.

Otho agreed to a sham marriage with Poppaea Sabina, forcing her to divorce her husband. This allowed Nero, who was infatuated with her, access. Yet Otho seduced her and even at times left Nero standing outside begging to be let in. It is instructive to consider Nero's response. He didn't force the matter or have Otho executed. Rather he was eventually rewarded

Figure 41: Bust of Galba. (Wikimedia Commons)

the governorship of Lusitania. We are told that he governed for ten years with 'moderation and restraint'. Whatever his feelings for Nero may have once been, he was one of the first to support Galba.

His description is of a slim man of moderate height, 'splay-footed and bandy-legged', almost feminine in his care of his person. He took great care of his appearance, plucking his body hair and shaving every day. A wig covered his thinning hair. An unlikely military commander, nothing about his life, as we shall see, hinted at the almost heroic ending of it. In the year 68 he was 36. Whilst he supported Galba, he could draw support from Nero's supporters although that was hardly a ringing endorsement for many in Rome.

The third in the line of contenders was Vitellius. Aulus Vitellius was born on 24 September 15. His father, Lucius Vitellius, had been a close advisor to Claudius. Consul three times, Nero had made him proconsul of Africa in the year 61-2. Galba, fatefully, was to appoint him governor in Germania Inferior, arriving there in November of 68. He was 53 when his troops proclaimed him emperor two months later.

Above left: Figure 42: Bust of Otho. (Wikimedia Commons)

Above right: Figure 43: Bust of Vitellius. (Wikimedia Commons)

He had held a prominent position in court, sharing Caligula's love of chariot racing and a passion for gambling under Claudius. However, he was said to be closer to Nero, ingratiating himself with the new emperor by flattering his musical ability. Unlike Vespasian, he was wise enough to never be caught falling asleep. During this period, Suetonius tells us that he was 'corrupted by every kind of disgrace'. While governor of Africa, it was alleged that he stole gifts and ornaments from temples and replaced others with fake copies made from tin and brass.

Tacitus described him as 'the slave and chattel of luxury and gluttony'. Unusually tall, with a red face from drinking and a protruding belly, one of his thighs was crippled from a chariot race he had been attending when Caligula was racing.

The fourth of the contenders was, of course, Vespasian and it is interesting to compare the four. The elderly Galba, arthritic, occasionally cruel yet perhaps the only man to match Vespasian militarily. The youngest, Otho, hardly a warrior himself but politically astute and well connected. Finally, Vitellius, 53 years old, corrupt, gluttonous and crippled by an old injury. On paper the battle-hardened, experienced Vespasian had the advantage. He also had a formidable army, one that had been tasting victory in Judea. However, Vespasian would be a late contender to this game of thrones.

Figure 44: Bust of Vespasian.
(Wikimedia Commons)

The Year of the Four Emperors

Back in spring 68, as Vespasian carved his way across Judea, Nero's reign was growing ever more unpopular. He was already on shaky ground. A great fire in Rome in 64 had placed huge financial demands on the state's coffers. The emperor's increasingly despotic regime was marked by an increase in trials, executions and forced exiles. New and increased taxes were imposed, estates confiscated and the coinage debased. Two plots against his life had already taken place before the Jewish revolt. By the time Vespasian set foot in the province the relationship between Nero and the senate had deteriorated. All the time, wagging tongues implicated Nero in the death of his own mother, as well as guilt by association concerning Claudius and Britannicus.

In spring 68, Gaius Julius Vindex, governor of Gallia Lugdunensis, rebelled against the emperor. He didn't want the throne for himself, so he looked for support, writing to a number of provincial governors. One of the few to reply was Servius Sulpicius Galba, governor of Hispania Tarraconensis, the largest of the Spanish provinces and home to the Sixth Legion, which eventually would serve in northern Britain. In April 68 Galba accepted Vindex's proposal and was declared emperor by his troops.

Nero sent Lucius Verginius Rufus, governor of Germania Superior, against Vindex. The armies met outside Vesontio, eastern Gaul. An initial talk found the two men on the verge of agreeing to join forces and removing Nero. However, the Rhine legions wanted blood and attacked the unprepared rebel troops, leaving 20,000 dead and Vindex committing suicide. They promptly proclaimed Virginius emperor, which he declined. Despite this initial victory, Nero began to leak support whilst Galba strengthened his position in Hispania.

The tipping point came when the prefect of the Praetorian Guard persuaded his men to abandon Nero and support Galba. On 9 June, the senate declared Nero an enemy of the state and proclaimed Galba emperor. Nero tried to flee in disguise but was recognised and forced to return to the palace. Cassius Dio claims he killed himself uttering the famous last words: 'Jupiter, what an artist perishes in me!' Suetonius tells us that, with the sound of horsemen drawing near to arrest him, he drove a dagger into his own throat with the help of his secretary, Epaphroditus.

The 71-year-old Galba was still in Spain when he was declared emperor by the senate. The new emperor seemed to have enjoyed great support at first, but the manner of his rule soon changed perceptions. He secured the Spanish provinces before arriving in Rome in October, after what Tacitus calls a 'long and bloody march' because of all the opponents he had killed. Here, perhaps, we see the seeds of his downfall at the very beginning of his short reign.

The praetorian prefect had promised the guards 30,000 sesterces each for changing their allegiance from Nero to Galba, a promise the new emperor had no intention of honouring. In addition, he refused the surrender of *Legio I Adiutrix*, formed by Nero, and killed thousands before demanding decimation, a practice not carried out since Tiberius.

His mistreatment of his opponents, and even some of his own supporters, soon left him with little support. He set about recovering gifts and monies given out by Nero whilst, at the same time, he allowed corruption in his own followers. He soon 'provoked the hostility of every section of Roman society.' It was perhaps his handling of the army in particular that proved his undoing.

A stern disciplinarian, he refused to pay customary donatives, stating his habit was to levy troops not to buy them. On 1 January the Rhine legions refused to swear allegiance and, instead, the very next day proclaimed their governor Aulus Vitellius emperor. Rome held its breath as a new civil war looked inevitable. Galba's response was to declare a certain Piso Frugi Licinianus his heir, believing this might shore up some support.

Into the narrative steps Marcus Salvius Otho. The 36-year-old senator was a very different person to Galba. A personal confidant of Nero, he was said to have been one of the late emperor's 'foremost friends … party to all Nero's schemes and secrets'. He had even agreed to marry Poppaea Sabina. Poppaea was already Nero's mistress and the marriage was a sham to remove her from her then husband, who was forced to divorce her. It appears Otho formed a genuine attachment to Poppaea but he, too, was forced to divorce her. Nero married her soon after Claudia was killed.

How Otho felt about Poppaea's subsequent death, apparently at the hands of Nero, may have been the main reason he was one of the first to turn against his former friend and support Galba. However, there was a second potential reason for Otho's change of heart. He had hoped to be recognised as Galba's heir. The sudden turn of events in the early days of 69 caused him to make a fateful decision.

Within two weeks Galba was assassinated in a plot orchestrated by Otho. His heir, Piso, was also killed. The Praetorians had been bribed for their support. Lured into the Forum, Galba was attacked, hacked down and his head placed on a spike. Otho was declared emperor by the senate but his reign was already in grave danger. Vitellius had sent half his powerful army, some of the best legions in the empire, into Italy.

Rather than avoid civil war Galba's death had merely replaced one of the combatants. Otho attempted to negotiate but Vitellius rebuffed him. Bloodshed seemed unavoidable. At Bedriacum the two armies met on 14 April. In a bloody encounter which left 40,000 dead, the Rhine legions were victorious. Otho was urged to fight on but instead chose suicide to save further bloodshed. In his death, 'so at odds with the manner of his life', he earned the respect of many Romans.

Aulus Vitellius marched triumphally into Rome. Tacitus described Vitellius as 'the slave and chattel of luxury and gluttony'. Suetonius labelled him 'corrupted by every type of disgrace'. He had been on good terms with Caligula, Claudius and Nero, sharing their passions for chariot racing, gambling and music respectively. Galba had appointed him governor in Lower Germany, apparently stating 'no one is to be feared who only thought of their stomach'. But it wasn't Vitellius that the new emperor needed to worry about, but the soldiers.

The Rhine legions were already badly disposed towards Galba. They felt they had not received their just rewards for putting down Vindex's revolt. Within a month of Vitellius's arrival they had refused to acclaim the new emperor sitting in Rome. Vitellius was only too happy to accept their support. The troops in Upper Germany followed suit.

The news of Galba's death made little difference. The die was cast. Otho had made attempts to avoid conflict. He had offered to share the empire and even to marry Vitellius's daughter. Those offers were rebuffed and Otho's defeat allowed the third emperor in 'the year of the four emperors' to take the throne. He proved as bloodthirsty as Galba had been in his treatment of opponents. He even killed those who had named him as heir to inherit the money. Worse was his treatment of the economy. Lavish banquets and parades drained the coffers as quickly as his support.

Meanwhile, Vespasian had been systematically bringing Judea back under Roman authority. He halted his advance on Jerusalem after hearing of Nero's death in June 68, sending Titus to receive instructions from Galba in the autumn. Galba kept Vespasian in position, perhaps fearing it a dangerous move to try to remove someone with such a large army under his command. But Galba did remove Sabinus, Vespasian's brother, from the Prefecture of the City and Titus lost a promised consulship.

On Galba's death Sabinus had been reinstated by Otho but events were clearly moving fast and Vespasian perhaps now began to ponder his own prospects. The war in the east dragged on but it would appear Vespasian halted operations when he heard of Vitellius's march on Rome in early 69. On Otho's death Sabinus, still in Rome, was forced to take the oath to Vitellius.

Back in Judea, the cautious Vespasian weighed his options. He found support from Licinius Mucianus in Syria and Tiberius Alexander who held the prefecture of Egypt. Crucially, the powerful Danubian legions, previously loyal, to Otho, did not favour Vitellius. Just over two months later, on 1 July, Vespasian was proclaimed emperor in Egypt. The emperor-elect sent his general Mucianus ahead with a formidable force which was soon backed up by declarations from the Balkan legions. Messages criss-crossed the empire searching for and offering support.

Both sides could have, and probably should have, waited for reinforcements. Vitellius had the support of many legions in the west, such as Britain and the Rhine. Vespasian remained in the east with a still-considerable army. It was the Flavians who struck first, invading northern Italy before Vitellius could rally further support. The Flavian army hadn't even waited for Mucianus to arrive. Instead, the Danube legions thrust into northern Italy. They very nearly ran into disaster. Fortunately for the Flavians, the Vitellian army was in some disorganisation as we shall see below. The two forces met near the site of Otho's defeat a few months before. A second battle of Bedriacum was soon to begin.

The Year of the Four Emperors was about to come to a bloody conclusion. It is useful at this point to note the positions of the legions spread across the empire. As we shall see many of those legions, or their detachments, fought at Bedriacum.

Table 2: The location of the legions c. 69

Province	Legions
Iberia	I Adiutrix VI Victrix X Gemina
Britannia	II Augusta VIIII Hispania XX Valeria Victrix XIV Gemina
Germania Inferior	XV Primigenia XVI Gallica I Germania
Germania Inferior	Macedonica XXII Primigenia
Pannonia	VII Galbiana XIII Gemina
Dalmatia	XI Claudia pia fidelis
Moesia	VII Claudia pia fidelis III Gallica VIII Augusta
Italy	I Italica V Alaudae XXI Rapax
Judea	V Macedonica X Frentensis XV Apollinaris
Syria	III Scythica VI Ferrata XII Fulminata
Egypt	III Cyrenaica XXII Deiotariana
Africa	I Macriana III Augusta liberatrix

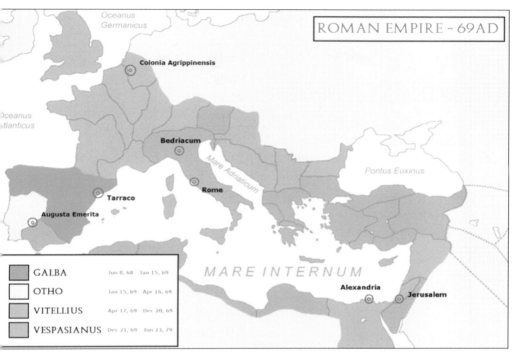

Figure 45: Map of the Roman Empire 68-9. (Wikimedia Commons)

The Battle of Bedriacum, 24 October, AD 69

With Vespasian's declaration the empire was essentially split in two. The western provinces largely supported Vitellius with those in the east backing Vespasian. Crucially, the Balkan legions had sided with the latter and they were much closer to events in Rome. Vespasian headed for Egypt to secure the strategically important Northern African provinces and their vital grain supplies, on which Rome largely depended. He sent his general Mucianus ahead of him, which meant an enormous 3,000-mile trek from Syria north-west through the Cicilian gates and across the Hellespont.

It was considered wiser for the Pannonian legions to hold the Alpine passes until Mucianus arrived. Vitellius had more legions and was getting support from Britannia and Germania. But one man urged a quick strike before Vitellius could muster his forces. Marcus Antonius Primus, legate of Legio VII Galbiana, convinced his fellow legates to push forward into northern Italy. After some initial successes, the Flavian army met their enemy about 250 miles north of Rome.

The Vitellian army in Italy was essentially leaderless. Their commander, Caecina, had attempted to defect to Vespasian and was thrown in jail. His intended replacement, the elderly Fabius Valens, fell ill and could not travel. Antonius Primus was an aggressive but tactically experienced commander. He sensed a window of opportunity before more legions arrived from across the Alps, and while the Vitellian army was without a commander. Yet he made a near-fatal error. Having reinforced Bedriacum, he sent auxiliary cohorts ahead and personally led 4,000 cavalry to reconnoitre.

At around 11 o'clock in the morning, about eight miles from the town of Cremona, where Caecina was held in chains, Antonius ran straight into the vanguard of two full legions. An initial Flavian charge pushed them back but the weight of numbers on the Vitellian side nearly caused a rout in the Flavian force. Antonius Primus rallied his men and formed a ragged battle line with his available auxiliaries and cavalry on the flanks. The Vitellians came on piecemeal and were driven back again. More men arrived from Cremona and Antonius likewise sent for reinforcements from Bedriacum some sixteen miles to his rear. Eventually, two battle lines began to form some four miles from Cremona.

The bulk of the Flavian legionaries arrived by late afternoon but they had few rations and most just carried their shields and weapons. By then, the Vitellians had formed a strong battle line and were well supplied from their camp just two miles behind, and the town of Cremona another two miles behind that. In addition, townspeople brought food and drink to the soldiers. The early advantage was for Vitellius.

A single road, the Via Postumia, ran between Bedriacum and Cremona, on a piece of raised land. Antonius laid his men out in a line that crossed the road. On his left flank he placed VII Claudia and VII Galbiana and on his right VIII Augusta and II Gallica. The Thirteenth Gemina and Praetorian cohorts held the centre. The enemy forces were of a similar size, just over 25,000 men. Contingents from nine legions blocked the Flavians' path to Cremona. Auxiliary cavalry held the flanks and rear of both armies.

The wisest policy for the Vitellians might have been to wait in Cremona for reinforcements and allow the Flavians to stand ready

the Gemonian stairs, where Galba had met his end, he was beaten and insulted, his last words recorded as 'Yet I was your emperor!' Domitian, who had been hiding in the city, had escaped the mob and was now hailed 'Caesar' by the crowds as his father's son. The following day the senate proclaimed Vespasian emperor.

Table 3: Timeline of the Year of the four Emperors

Emperor	Date	Comments
Nero	Early 68	Vindex, legate of Gallia Lugdunensis, rebelled, encouraged Galba to join him and offered Galba his support for the throne. Defeated at Vesontio in Gaul by Rhine legions and committed suicide.
	April 68	Galba, legate of Hispania Terraconensis, declared Emperor.
Galba	9 June 68	Senate proclaims Galba emperor and declares Nero enemy of the state. Nero commits suicide.
	October 68	Galba enters Rome
	1 January 69	Rhine legions refuse to swear allegiance to Galba.
	2 January 69	Rhine legions declare Vitellius emperor.
Otho	15 January 69	Galba murdered. Otho declared emperor.
	14 April 69	Battle of Bedriacum. Vitellius defeats Otho who commits suicide.
Vitellius	19 April 69	Vitellius declared emperor
	1 July 69	Vespasian declared emperor in Egypt.
	24 October 69	Second battle of Bedriacum. Army of Vitellius defeated.
	20 December 69	Flavian army enters Rome and Vitellius is killed.
Vespasian	21 December 69	Senate declares Vespasian emperor

Meanwhile Vespasian was still in Egypt. The new emperor inherited a number of problems. Aside from nearly two years of civil conflict, the empire had suffered years of misgovernment by Nero. The war in Judea dragged on, tying up significant numbers of troops in the east. In addition, a major revolt along the Rhine had erupted and was in full swing on Vespasian's accession.

Batavian revolt 69-70

The Batavi were a Germanic tribe situated around the Rhine delta. They had supplied the Roman army with significant numbers of auxiliary troops. Some units had accompanied Plautius and Vespasian in the invasion of Britain. It is thought it was a Batavian unit which swam across the Medway, and later the Thames, in the two dramatic battles previously discussed. A sub-tribe of the Chatti, they were located in the province of Germania Inferior. They provided a disproportionate number of troops compared to their population of around 35,000; one cavalry *ala* and eight infantry cohorts numbered nearly 5,000 men, as large as a single legion.

Their prince, Gaius Julius Civilis, had served as a *praefectus* for twenty-five years, part of which were in Britain. The units were removed from Britain in 66 and Civilis and his brother were later caught up in Roman political intrigues and found themselves arrested, possibly falsely, by the governor of Germania Inferior. His brother, a non-citizen, was executed but Civilis had the protection of Roman law and was sent to the capital in chains. It was whilst awaiting his fate in AD 69 that Nero was overthrown and the new emperor, Galba, installed. Galba acquitted Civilis who returned home, no doubt resenting his ill-treatment and his brother's death.

Civilis was soon arrested again, this time by a new governor. At the same time, Galba dismissed his German bodyguards, which included several hundred battle-hardened Batavians. To make matters worse, relations deteriorated between the Batavian auxiliaries and Legio XIV Gemina, to which they had been attached for meany years. Throughout 69 tensions resulted in fights between the German auxiliaries and Roman legionaries. Civilis remained in prison when Galba was murdered and replaced by Otho in early 69. Vitellius had Civilis released in return for

Batavian help in his defeat of Otho. In summer 69 a final insult pushed the Batavians into open rebellion.

Desperate for troops in light of Vespasian's advance the local governor, going against the treaty, tried to conscript more Batavians and refused others their discharge. This proved to be the last straw for the Batavians. Four emperors in quick succession had proved to be untrustworthy masters: Nero, Galba, Otho and now Vitellius. Civilis masterminded an attack on several forts at once, aided by the Cananefates tribe to the north. A relief force of auxiliaries was sent against them but was defeated near Arnhem. Two legions and three auxiliary units were next to be ordered to suppress the revolt. Crucially, one was a Batavian cavalry ala and, seeing their comrades, they defected. The Romans were defeated and forced to retreat to their base at Castra Vetera (Xanten).

Civilis was hell-bent on revenge and besieged the two legions at Vetera. Meanwhile, the defeat of Vitellius threw the Rhine legions into confusion. Civilis took full advantage and broke the siege to attack towards Krefeld and the main base in Germania Superior, Moguntiacum. When Vespasian became emperor, the Batavians renewed the siege at Vetera. The legionaries had resorted to eating their horses and mules and were eventually starved out. A promise of safe conduct proved worthless as the defeated Romans were ambushed and massacred a short distance from their abandoned fort. The camp was looted. The Romans had been forced to leave their artillery and weapons behind and the experienced Batavians then had a significant amount of booty. Further tribes joined them.

Vespasian had inherited a major revolt. The new emperor appointed Quintus Petillius Cerialis as commander and eight legions were sent to quell the Batavians. Six of those legions launched an offensive towards Castra Vetera: VI Victrix; II Adriutrix; XXI Rapax; XIV Gemina; I Germanica and XVI Gallica. The subsequent battle lasted two days.

A wide marshy plain separated the armies and the first day's confused fighting proved inconclusive. Fought near the fortress on a plain beside the Rhine, on the second day the Roman general Cerialis formed up in two lines. Civilis had built a dam diverting the water onto the 'naturally marshy' area. Tacitus provided some details starting with the first day of the battle:[4] 'there was no fighting at close quarters, as is usual in an engagement between infantry, but the struggle was rather like a naval fight, for the men floundered about in the water.' The next day Cerialis posted his cavalry and auxiliary infantry in the front line with his legions behind, keeping 'picked troops' back under his own leadership for emergencies.

The Batavians placed their troops in columns rather than an extended front, the Batavi and Cugerni were on his right; the left wing, nearer the river, was held by tribes from across the Rhine. Tacitus describes the two generals talking to their troops and claims Cerialis reminded the Sixth that it was 'by their influence that Galba had been made emperor' and urged his troops to regain their former camp which the Batavians held.

The Germans, with 'clashing arms and wild dancing according to their custom', opened battle with a volley of missiles, including stones and leaden balls. But the Romans refused the provocation and were not lured onto the marshy ground. The Germans were forced to attack and pushed back the auxiliary troops, only for the legions, including the Sixth, to enter the fray and stop the advance. The two lines locked together and vicious hand-to-hand fighting ensued.

It was a Batavian deserter who apparently swung the balance to the Romans. He led two troops of Roman cavalry round the marsh and behind the Batavians. On a signal, the cavalry attacked the rear and the legions charged, routing the enemy. Only heavy rain and nightfall saved the Batavians from complete destruction.

The victory was commemorated in an inscription that mentions the new emperor, Vespasian, and the commander of the Sixth Legion, Sextus Caelius Tuscus:[5]

to the son of imperator Vespasian
Augustus, with tribunician
powers, imperator for the
fourth time, twice consul, appointed
for a third term, appointed as censors,
to Aulus Marius Celsus,
governor with the rank of propraetor,
and to Sextus Caelius Tuscus,
commander, [this was monument dedicated by]
the Sixth legion
Victrix

Summary

Vespasian's rise to power was unexpected. Under different circumstances his career may have ended in the early years of Nero's reign, fading into obscurity and retirement. Even when back in favour with Nero, his inability to show consistent enthusiastic support for the emperor's artistic pursuits could have brought his career, or even his life, to an abrupt halt. The Jewish revolt of 66 presented Nero with an urgent problem. He needed someone competent enough to deal with the situation, but not too popular or influential to present a threat. Vespasian's relative obscurity was perhaps a major factor in Nero's decision.

Then in his late fifties, Vespasian probably viewed this as potentially his last military campaign. The death of Nero in 68 probably came as a surprise but he was quick to offer Galba his support. It is not known when Vespasian considered his own position. Perhaps it was when Vitellius was declared emperor by the Rhine legions at the beginning of 69. However, the first signs of Flavian ambitions occurred when Titus was en route to Rome to negotiate with Galba. At Corinth in early February Titus learnt of Galba's death and Otho's accession two weeks before.

Galba had dismissed Sabinus from the Prefecture of the City. In theory, Titus's mission was to gain support for his candidature for praetorship and for a continuation of his father's campaign in Judea. Otho reinstated Sabinus but Titus did not continue to Rome. Fearing he would become hostage to either Otho or Vitellius, he returned to Judea. According to Tacitus, it was at that point that the Flavians looked to their own ambitions and made preparations.

At Caesarea in the east the army had sworn allegiance to Otho who also had support from the Danubian legions. When Otho killed himself after the battle of Bedriacum there were many who looked for a rival to support against Vitellius. It would appear that Vespasian hesitated and it was in fact his son, Titus, and his generals, such as Mucianus, who were more hawkish. In June Vespasian consulted the oracle of Ba'al and had a meeting with Mucianus. The die was cast on 1 July when Julius Alexander addressed the two legions based at Nicopolis. Crowds in Alexandria were equally enthusiastic in their endorsement. Two days later, at Vespasian's headquarters in Caesarea, the duty guard addressed their general as 'imperator' the traditional greeting given to new emperors.

It was a remarkable turn of events. Just three years before Vespasian was in forced retirement. His successful campaign in Judea might have been his last role in civic life. But in just ten months Nero, Galba and Otho had all perished. Vespasian found himself in the right place and time with a huge army at his disposal and significant support across the empire. That he waited several months before making his move demonstrates that he was a thoughtful, prudent man, qualities that would stand him in good stead during his reign.

Figure 47: Bust of Vespasian. (Wikimedia commons)

Chapter 6

THE COLOSSEUM, VESPASIAN'S GREATEST MONUMENT

Perhaps one of Vespasian's greatest legacies was construction of Rome's iconic arena. It forms the backdrop to a long-awaited TV gladiator series, *Those About to Die*, starring Anthony Hopkins. Based on a book of the same name by Daniel P. Mannix, hopefully it will bring to life the reality of gladiatorial contests and political intrigues during the reign of Vespasian, played by Hopkins.

Originally called simply 'The Amphitheatre' or 'The Hunting Theatre', it only earned the title Colosseum in medieval times. Construction began around AD 72. Nero had suffered the fate of many a fallen emperor, *damnatio memoriae*. Vespasian's decision to build a new stone amphitheatre on the site of Nero's *Domus Aurea* (Golden Palace) was thus a popular one. It signalled the return of public land to the people, land that many regarded as having been stolen by his hated predecessor. Much of the costs were funded by the spoils from the Jewish War and the sack of the temple in Jerusalem.

Completed just after Vespasian's death, it was dedicated under Titus in AD 80. It rose three storeys above the ground, to which Domitian added a fourth taking it to forty-five metres high. Canvas awnings, the *valeria*, were supported by wooden masts and 240 post holes around the top show where they were positioned. They were vital for the comfort of the crowd. At earlier games in a different arena Caligula, when he was feeling particularly cruel, delighted in having the canopy removed and watching people wilt under the sun, forbidding anyone to leave. We can see that such canopies were considered an asset as they were often depicted on leaflets and bills when advertising a show.

Seventy-six numbered entrances led to the seating areas. Four larger entrances, one on each side of the ellipse, were for the emperor, magistrates and performers. Once inside, a podium was set aside for the emperor, senators and ambassadors. Fourteen rows behind them were the equestrians in the *ima cavea*. Next came the *cives Romani* in the *media cavea*. Sub-divisions separated married men, boys under 17 who sat with their tutors and soldiers. Girls, young women and mothers sat in the gods way up high away from the gaze of the cheap seats below.

The dimensions were impressive, covering six acres.[1] The arena itself measured 84 by 54 metres (278 by 177 feet). In contrast the pitch at Wembley stadium is 105 by 69 metres. However, the arena floor is much closer to the size of an American football pitch, 91 by 53 metres. Four tiers of seats rose above, seating up to 87,000 spectators (estimates vary from a low of 50,000). In comparison, the current largest premiership stadium, Manchester United's Old Trafford, holds just over 74,000.

The Roman poet Martial witnessed the inaugural games in AD 80 and used all his rhetorical skills to rank it above all the ancient Wonders of the World. It became the model for other stone amphitheatres, with over 200 built across the empire over the following centuries. It is likely that many others were built of wood or were temporary and taken down after use. Thus, the majority are now lost to us. In Rome such temporary structures were common with the Forum often used as a location for games. The Circus Maximus, though primarily used for chariot races, was also used, with a stone structure dating from c. 200 BC.

The Theatre was a political as much as a sporting venue. As far as is known, there was no entrance price. It was provided to citizens at the largesse of the benefactor, usually the emperor. Tokens of wood, bone or lead suggest admission was restricted to certain classes and seating was tightly packed at forty centimetres per person and seventy centimetres leg room.[2] About a quarter of Rome's population of a million would have been adult males, half of whom were slaves. With a maximum capacity of 87,000, this would have accommodated two thirds of the free adult male population.

Figures 48 and 49 show the exterior and interior of the Colosseum today. By the time of Vespasian, the games were hugely popular. Let us turn to how these events evolved over the centuries.

Figure 48: Colosseum. (Wikimedia Commons)

Figure 49: Colosseum Interior. (Wikimedia Commons)

The historical background of gladiatorial games

By the first century, the Roman games, or *munus*, had become an integral part of social and political life in the Roman Empire. Gladiators were one part of this; however, the games themselves were much more than just gladiators. For example, a third-century festival of 176 days set aside 100 days for theatrical shows, sixty-four for horse and chariot racing and just ten for gladiatorial contests.[3] Yet their popularity and cultural significance were disproportionate to the time set aside in a festival or games.

It is likely that gladiatorial contests evolved from funeral games. Mural paintings of chariot races and athletic contests have been found in Etruscan tombs. An early example dated to c.370–340 BC depicts chariot races and boxing matches but, additionally, two fighters armed with spears, shields and helmets. Livy records gladiators fighting after the Samnite war in 327–304 BC. The first attested gladiatorial contest in Rome dates to 264 BC.[4] Three pairs of gladiators fought at funeral games to honour the deceased.

The next recorded example in 216 BC has twenty-two pairs of gladiators. This is the same year as the battle of Cannae when Hannibal destroyed a Roman army of 80,000 men during the Second Punic War. During his campaign he is said to have used captured tribesmen to fight for their freedom and entertain his troops.

But not all gladiators were prisoners of war or slaves. Livy provides an interesting example from Spain in 206 BC.[5] Whilst they were usually slaves or 'men who sell their blood', in this case they 'were all volunteers and gave their services gratuitously'. Sent by their chiefs, their main desire seems to have been to demonstrate their martial ability to the watching Roman general. In other situations, it was rivalry or to settle a score, suggesting one could choose one's adversary.

Gladiatorial contests had spread throughout the Italian peninsula by the second century BC becoming spectacles in their own right. They were no longer confined to funerals. Other forms of entertainment were also included such as beast hunts and, gruesomely, the execution of prisoners. Some of Rome's elite may have turned their noses up at this low form of 'entertainment': in 165 BC the Roman writer Terence complained that gladiator contests had become more popular than plays and other more highbrow forms of entertainment.[6] But the mob loved to be entertained and who, in 167 BC, could resist seeing a group of deserters being trampled to death by elephants?[7]

The rise in popularity meant more and more men were required. Gladiator schools appeared and it was one such school that led to the famous slave uprising led by Spartacus. The Third Servile War began in 73 BC when Spartacus led seventy gladiators to escape from a gladiator school in Capua. Runaway slaves from across the region swelled their ranks. The danger must have been thought significant as the Romans sent a force of 3,000 to besiege the rebel camp on Mount Vesuvius. The Romans blocked the only route down but foolishly neglected to set a proper camp. Sensing an opportunity, Spartacus led his men unseen down ropes to attack from a different direction. The captured Roman arms aided the cause, and it took two years before the revolt was crushed finally in 71 BC.

A few years later Julius Caesar owned his own gladiator school, also at Capua. It is estimated to have trained 5,000 fighters.[8] In one festival of games in 65 BC, Caesar paired 320 fighters in games to honour his father who had died twenty years earlier. The games had not only become separated from the actual funeral, they had also become more elaborate: in 46 BC, Caesar presented a mock battle involving 1,000 infantry, cavalry and even twenty war elephants. Pompey, Caesar's rival, had also used twenty elephants but with 600 lions and 410 leopards in one festival.[9] State-financed contests began after Caesar's death in 44 BC.[10]

Across the empire an average-sized games might consist of a dozen pairs of gladiators a day in a week-long festival. This was dwarfed by the events sponsored by emperors in Rome. Eager to curry favour and popularity with the mob, they put on increasingly extravagant spectacles. The first emperor, Augustus, is said to have recruited 10,000 fighters in eight enormous shows, over 1,000 gladiators in each. Augustus himself claimed that 3,500 animals were killed.

Caligula showed his cruelty by throwing prisoners to wild beasts and forcing others to fight to the death. The distinction between professional gladiators and prisoners is made clear by Seneca who records the latter having 'no defensive armour … helmet or shield'.[11] Seneca also described the programme of a day's entertainment: in the morning they 'throw men to the lions and the bears'. In this instance, every fight ended in death by fire or sword. Perhaps he was referring to executions as he comments that this occurred even when the arena was empty.

Claudius, a lover of gladiator contests, celebrated the conquest of Britain with a depiction of an assault and sacking of a town in AD 44. Suetonius states this was held in the Campus Martius, a 490-acre site in the north-west of the city: 'in the Campus Martial he staged the siege and destruction of a town, in the manner of an actual war, and also the surrender of the kings of the Britons.' All the while wearing a legate's cloak. Could this be one of Vespasian's victories? It's more likely to be the capture of Camulodunum as it featured the surrender of kings of the Britons. It seems clear Claudius was taking the credit there.

Suetonius went on to describe his cruel and bloodthirsty nature: if any fighter fell to the ground he ordered his death, particularly net-fighters as they were un-helmeted and he could see their faces as they died. He was particularly fond of animal hunts and would often commit men to the beasts on the most trivial pretext. An unlucky attendant or workman could find himself in the arena for a spilt drink or malfunctioning scenery. One of his ushers was sent to the arena still wearing his toga.

Not all subsequent emperors loved the games. Antoninus Pius and his successor, Marcus Aurelius, abhorred them. In contrast, Lucius Verus had a great passion for them. Hadrian also enjoyed them and was said to have been skilled in combat. Beast hunts were an especial favourite and during his birthday celebrations he is said to have killed 200 lions.[12]

But it is Commodus who outdid them all with his passion for the games. He took part in over 1,000 gladiatorial contests, many while his father was still alive. His preferred type was a *secutor*, armed with a heavy shield, armour, distinctive helmet and a gladius or short sword. The normal opponent would be the lightly-armoured *retiarus*. The retiarus was armed with a net, trident and dagger. This passion was to prove his undoing. His insistence in competing in front of the mob was considered scandalous and unbecoming an emperor. His advisors begged him to reconsider but he dismissed them angrily and planned their executions. That decision would lead to his death, strangled in his bath at the age of 31. The fascinating story of Commodus and his gladiatorial exploits feature in the book, *The Real Gladiator*, which covers the history behind the 2000 film.

Any association with funerary ceremonies had now completely disappeared and they were extravagant spectacles to enhance prestige and entertain the mob. Traditionally, they were held twice a year, in December and March. In the fourth century the growth of Christianity and the policies of Constantine I caused their demise, although they continued in reduced form for some time in the West. At the beginning of the fifth century the Western emperor Honorius prohibited them for good.

Back in the first century, gladiators became so popular that even freemen would risk their lives in search of glory. In 38 BC the senate had formally to ban those of the senatorial class taking part. It is probable that many a senator had a son eager for adventure but, whatever the case, it is interesting that such legislation was required. In 22 BC a decree banned equestrians as well. Yet young men of rank continued to be eager to compete, even if the social and cultural attitudes were against the practice. Women were also banned, implying that some shows had allowed them to take part. However, in AD 11 new legislation was introduced, once again allowing equestrians and free-born men over the age of 25 to enter. Interestingly, free-born women over the age of 20 were also allowed.[13]

By AD 19 the senate changed their mind and once again banned senators or equestrians taking part, although later both Caligula and Nero reversed this. Augustus had limited games to two *munera* a year with a maximum of 120 gladiators and by the Flavian period only the emperor or appointed official could stage one in Rome. It became customary to set aside ten days at the end of December for such events.

Outside the city chief magistrates of a region or town were expected to provide four days of spectacles for the citizens.[14] The Greek-speaking areas of the East and the North African provinces were just as fond of gladiatorial spectacles.[15] Beast hunts were extremely popular and there was a thriving trade between North Africa and the rest of the empire in wild animals. Private hunting corporations were common throughout the empire.[16] Huge quantities of animals were captured and transported across the Mediterranean. When the Colosseum opened in AD 80, in games lasting over a hundred days, 9,000 'beasts' were killed.[17]

Beast hunters and executions

As games evolved it became traditional to begin the day's entertainment with beast hunts. Some performances were little more than circus acts with ostriches, monkeys and even sea lions. Larger animals, such as giraffes and hippopotamuses, must have caused significant logistical difficulties in transportation. The star attractions were the more dangerous animals. Bears, lions, tigers, bulls, elephants, crocodiles and even rhinoceroses. In 2 BC, twenty-six crocodiles and 260 lions were killed in two separate events in Rome.[18] They could be caused to fight each other as well as men.

The men pitched against these animals were called *venatores*, the beast hunters. In the second century the *venatores* tended to be unarmoured and wore a simple tunic whilst armed with a spear. Lower than the *venatores* were the *bestiarii*. These men were unarmed and attempted to provoke the animals. An example of this, *taurocatapsia*, ancient Cretan bull wrestling, was introduced by Julius Caesar. A rider would overtake the bull and jump on its back, pulling it to the ground by its horns. Generally, hunters used javelins or bows, either on foot or mounted. Some individual animals gained a reputation and were given nicknames and saved from death.[19] Elephants were very popular; at one games organised by Pompey they were forced to fight and seemed to beg for mercy, moving the audience to tears.[20]

Criminals who were thrown to the beasts were *damnatus ad bestias*, 'condemned by animal'. We can see how ritualised the games were by how they performed executions. Mythological and historical stories were re-enacted.[21] One example comes from the story of Pasiphae, wife of King Minos of Crete. The god Poseidon wished to punish the king and made his wife fall in love with a bull, resulting in the birth of the Minotaur. Martial writes: 'Pasiphae was coupled with the Dictaean bull; we have seen it, the ancient tale has now been proved … whatever fame sings of, the arena tenders to you.' There is no way of knowing how the Romans presented this. Was there a real bull? Were there two actors? Or perhaps this formed part of a woman's grisly punishment?

Another example comes from the myth of Prometheus. Punished for stealing the secret of fire from the gods, he was tied to a rock. Lying there helpless, an eagle devoured his liver only for it to regrow and the terrible punishment to repeated every day. Martial again: 'Laureolus, hanging from a cross that was no stage-prop, offer up his uncovered entrails to a Caledonian bear. His torn joints carried on living as his limbs dripped, and in all his flesh, no flesh remained'. It seems that the condemned Laureolus was hung from a cross and then a bear set on him. Perhaps his stomach opened to encourage the beast. Mercifully quicker than a prolonged death from crucifixion. One wonders what crime deserved such a punishment?

In the reign of Augustus, a Sicilian bandit named Selurus earned a similar fate.[22] Operating around Mount Etna for some years, Selerus was eventually captured alive. A wooden apparatus symbolising the mountain was constructed with cages full of wild animals underneath. The audience would be able to see Selurus on top of his mountain stronghold and no doubt also the fate awaiting him below. Selerus may not have had a good view of what was beneath him, but the sounds would have been unmistakable.

He certainly knew when he entered the arena that he would not be coming out alive. No doubt a dramatic build up raised the tension until a trapdoor opened, plunging the condemned Selerus into the cages below. Perhaps if Spartacus had been captured alive, he, too, would have endured such a death. Unable to find his body, the Romans crucified 6,000 prisoners along the Appian Way between Rome and Capua.

Examples of executions under Nero were particularly gruesome;[23] criminals wrapped in animal skins were mauled to death by dogs; prisoners were crucified by day and burned alive at night; and a certain Meniscus, perhaps only guilty of theft, was dressed as Hercules and burned alive. Caligula and Claudius were both keen fans of the *venatio* and regularly threw people to the beasts for entertainment.[24] Cassius Dio, writing over a century and a half later, noted that Caligula was 'ruled by charioteers and gladiators' and was a 'slave of actors'. He caused a scandal by forcing Roman citizens to fight with twenty-six equestrians killed on one occasion. Claudius also had an 'excessive fondness' for the games with 300 bears and a similar number of *Africanae*, probably lions, being killed between chariot races.

Commodus regularly took part in beast hunts. Sometimes a safety platform was built around the arena to allow him to shoot down in safety. Skilled with both the bow and javelin, on one occasion he decapitated an ostrich on the run with a crescent-shaped arrow. In ad 70, 2,500 captured Jews were forced into team combats, thrown to the beasts or burned alive.[25] In Athens, thousands of beasts, including 100 lions, were killed. Perhaps the bloodiest display was provided by Trajan after his Dacian campaigns (AD 101-106). In games lasting 123 days, 11,000 animals were killed and 10,000 gladiators fought.[26] Titus, celebrating the opening of the Colosseum in AD 80, had 5,000 animals killed in the first 100 days and a further 4,000 over the entire spectacle.

We get an idea of the day's events at a *munus* from literary sources:[27] Beast hunts in the morning, public executions during the lunch break, the star attractions, the gladiators, in the afternoon. It is to these latter that we next turn. Their reputation and fame continued long after the empire ended. By the time of Vespasian, they had evolved into distinct types with specific matches preferred. Those were carefully planned and matched contests. A referee, *summa rudis*, 'first stick', made sure rules were adhered to.

Types of gladiator

This chapter introduced us to gladiatorial contests within the context of games. Those fights could be viewed as the main attraction. The closest modern comparison is perhaps boxing, although we'd have to place a series of bouts at the end of a day's circus entertainments and executions to get a closer analogy. As in boxing, a fight between gladiators had a referee, a *summa rudis*, 'first stick'. Several other important people ensured the smooth running of the games:[28]

> *Editor*: Official or citizen funding the spectacle.
> *Aedile*: Responsible for supervising public games and maintenance of streets and buildings.
> *Lanista*: Trainer and manager of gladiators and gladiator schools.
> *Familia*: Group of arena performers.
> *Summa rudis*: Senior referee.
> *Secunda rudis*: Junior referees.

Early images from the fourth century BC depict fighters wearing a simple loincloth, their only protection a helmet and round hoplite type shield. Each was armed with a spear. Leg greaves appear in later periods and specific types of gladiator began to evolve. By the republican period there were several different types: *scissor*, *eques*, *thraex*, *myrmillo*, *retiarius*, *sagittarius*, *veles*, *hoplomachus*, *samnis* and *gallus*.[29] By Vespasian's reign the main types of gladiator can be seen in table 4.

Table 4: Main types of gladiator[30]

Gladiator	Description
Hoplomachus	Small round shield, broad-rimmed visored helmet with a crest and a feather on either side. High greaves on legs and *manica* on his right arm. Bare-chested with loincloth and belt. Trousers gave some protection to the thighs. Armed with spear and dagger or short sword. Often paired with a *myrmillo* or *thraex*.
Thraex	Similar to a *hoplomachus* with loincloth and leg coverings. Griffin-crested helmet symbolising goddess of retribution. Carried a smaller square, curved shield, 2-feet wide. High greaves and *manica* on right arm. Armed with a *sica*, a short, curved dagger, Often paired with a myrmillo or a hoplomachus.
Myrmillo	Broad-rimmed, visored helmet with fish-shaped crest and tail decorated with a plume of feathers. Greave protected the left leg only, and *manica* on right arm. Armed with a gladius sword and *scutum* shield. The shield was 3 feet in length and protected from greave to chin. Classed as heavy gladiators, they carried forty pounds of equipment. Usually paired with thraex, hoplomachus or retiarius.
Retiarius	This is the iconic gladiator, armed with a *fuscina*, or trident. He was largely unarmoured with no helmet, shield or greaves. While other gladiator types wore a manica on their right arms the retiarius wore his on the left in which he held his weighted net. On his left shoulder he wore a *galerus*, a metal plate protecting the left shoulder, neck and head. He also carried a dagger as a backup. A *laquerarius* was similar but carried a lasso instead of a net. Both were the most lightly armed of the gladiators. A retiarius was often paired with a secutor, who was heavily armed. These were one of the most popular matched pairs throughout the imperial period.

Gladiator	Description
Secutor	Designed to fight the retiarius. Similar to a myrmillo with a large scutum shield, greave on left leg, *manica* on right arm and armed with a gladius. The helmet, however, was very different. It was smooth and streamlined with a fin-like crest to resemble a fish. The curved surface prevented the net catching and a visor with small eye holes stopped the points of the trident penetrating. The secutor tired quickly and the helmet restricted vision and oxygen. Also known as *contraretiarius*
Arbelas or scissor	Crested and visored helmet with scale or mail armour down to the knees. A *manica* protected the right arm and short greaves protected both legs up to the knees. No shield. In his right arm he carried a dagger but in his left was an unusual weapon. Looking rather like a type of pirate's hook, the *arbela* had a crescent-shaped blade, likely sharpened both sides. There was also what looks like a metal protective tube into which one placed his forearm with presumably a handle at the base or straps to hold into position. Often paired with *retiarius*.
Provocator	Wore a loincloth and belt along with a metal breast plate. The helmet had a neck guard covering the sides and back. He carried a rectangular shield, perhaps smaller than that of a *myrmillo* but wore a longer greave on his left leg. The principal weapon was a straight sword. Generally, paired with other provocators but one example shows against the heavier myrmillo.
Dimachaerus	Broad-rimmed, visored helmet. Greaves on both legs, no shield. Tunic or mail to protect torso. Carried two short swords, one possibly curved. Often paired with another dimachaerus.
Eques	Lightly-armoured, mounted gladiators with a round shield, 2 feet in diameter. Scale armour or tunic. Carried a 7-8-feet long spear and gladius. Visored-helmet often with feather each side. Only fought each other.

Other types of fighter also existed and many more are probably lost to history. The *gallus* was an early form of the *myrmillo*. He carried a *scutum* shield, greave and helmet. Armed with a gladius they had disappeared by the first century BC. The sagittarius was protected by a conical helmet and scale armour. His principal weapon, as his name suggests, was the bow. The *samnis* seems to have been confined to the republican era but Livy provides a good description. The shield was broad at the top and tapered to the bottom. They wore plumed-helmets, armour and a single greave on their left leg. A fighter wearing a multi-coloured tunic and protected by a gold-coloured shield fought an opponent with a silver shield and white tunic with spear and sword. Other sources suggest an oval shield and armour comprised of three metal discs.

A fascinating description by Tacitus portrays the *crupellarius* as completely covered in steel. They were slow moving and whilst 'ill-adapted for inflicting wounds, they were impenetrable to them'. It is possible these depicted a type of Gallic warrior. In AD 21 the Romans fought against a Gallic tribe, the Aedui, and encountered men in 'iron plates' that 'did not yield to javelins or swords'. The legionaries used hatchets, pickaxes, forked poles and pikes to beat them to the ground where they lay 'without any effort to rise like dead men'.[31]

The 2000 film *Gladiator* depicted chariots being used against infantry. Whilst this is not unlikely in a battle re-enactment, we have little evidence of chariot duels. Literary sources suggest an *essedarius* may have entered the arena armed with spear and round shield. It is perhaps more likely he dismounted to fight on foot. It is difficult to distinguish such examples from a *venatore* or *bestiarii*. It would have been possible to use chariots as a mobile platform from which to kill animals with bow or javelin. An interesting anecdote from Suetonius describes Claudius granting an *essadarius* a wooden sword, the symbol of his freedom, after the man's four sons had pleaded on his behalf. This, Claudius said, showed that people should have children as they brought 'support and favour even to a gladiator'.

A *veles* carried a shield, javelin and sword and appears to have resembled a light infantryman of the republic era. Another lightly-armed fighter was a *paegniarius* who carried a simple stick and a whip. With no armour or shield, the only protection was cloth wrapping on the arms and legs. They were especially popular under Commodus and were probably a warm-up act before the more traditional types.

Other types of 'warm-up' acts included the *cestus*, a type of boxer, although with a variety of different gloves, some simply padded, others wrapped in iron or even spikes. The *noxxi* weren't really gladiators at all but prisoners or criminals usually matched against animals. The *andabata* wore a special helmet with no eye holes at all. Fighting against another *andabata* the two blind fighters were protected by mail and would have flailed around to the delight of the crowd.

The iconic gladiators in Table 4 are perhaps the most commonly depicted in films. It is important to note that these were carefully matched against each other. The 'fisherman' *retiarius* tried to outwit and catch the more heavily-armoured *secutor* wearing the fish-adorned helmet. Here was matched the lightest armoured gladiator against a heavily armoured one; one with no shield but carrying a net and trident, the other with a large scutum shield, large helmet and gladius sword. No doubt there was an element of cat and mouse in the contest, the lighter gladiator attempting to either lure him into position to throw his net or to tire him out, the secutor attempting to close in to use his sword.

Spectators had their favourite type. Commodus trained to fight as a *secutor*. Domitian preferred the *myrmillo* fighters and, when a man spoke disparagingly about them in comparison with a *thraex*, the emperor threw him to the dogs in the arena to be torn apart, forced to wear a tag stating 'A buckler-wearer with a big mouth'. Table 5 shows the most common matches.

Table 5: Common gladiator pairs

Gladiator	Opponent
Secutor	Retiarius
Scissor or Arbelas	Retiarius
Thraex	Myrmillo, Hoplomachus
Hoplomachus	Myrmillo, Thraex
Retiarius	Secutor, Myrmillo, Scissor/Arbelas
Myrmillo	Thraex, Hoplomachus, Retiarius
Dimachaerus	Dimachaerus
Eques	Eques
Provocator	Provocator

In films gladiatorial contests are often displayed as a disorganised free-for-all with fighters wearing an assortment of weird and wonderful costumes. In *Gladiator*, Maximus and the other recruits are chained in pairs to fight a group of gladiators in a huge mêlée. Later, Maximus fights six opponents single-handedly, all armed and armoured with an odd assortment of helmets, armour and weapons. The last is wearing a pig-like helmet. In reality, the bouts were organised and, though designed to entertain, were expected to follow certain conventions. A referee would have ensured rules were respected. Figures 50 to 58 show an assortment of different gladiator types.

Figure 50:
Hoplomachus
vs Thraex.
(Wikimedia
Commons)

Figure 51: Thraex
vs Murmillo.
(Wikimedia
Commons)

Left: Figure 52: Provocator vs Provocator. (Wikimedia Commons)

Below: Figure 53: Retiarius vs Secutor. (Wikimedia Commons)

Figure 54: Scissor vs Retiarius. (Wikimedia Commons)

Figure 55: Eques vs Eques. (Wikimedia Commons)

Figure 56: Mounted eques. (Wikimedia Commons)

Above left: Figure 57: Gladiators fighting. (Alisa Vanlint)

Above right: Figure 58: Gladiators fighting. (Alisa Vanlint)

Life of a gladiator

Gladiators came from three main demographics: prisoners of war, slaves and criminals. The last, classed as *noxii*, were sentenced to *damnati ad gladium*. All three groups were outsiders from society and thus had no rights at all. However, some free-born men, plebeians or even equestrians, could choose to join their ranks, reflected in the term *infamia*, which meant a loss of status as well as citizens' rights.[32] Decrees in 46, 38, 22 BC and AD 19 forbade the elite of Roman society in taking part which demonstrates just how popular the allure of the arena could be.[33] The poor, destitute or bankrupt individuals saw success in the arena as a desperate way out. Socially, they were on the same social level as prostitutes and actors. From the first century BC, ex-gladiators were prohibited from holding office, serving on a jury or becoming a soldier.

The first step in their new life was often a *ludus*, training camp. Once there any free-born men were no longer protected from physical abuse or corporal punishment. Seneca records gladiators swearing an oath agreeing to be burned, chained up or killed.[34] The oath, *sacramentum gladiatorium*, is also recorded by Petronius (*Satyricon*, 117, 1st century) 'He vows to endure to be burned, to be bound, to be beaten, and to be killed by the sword': *uri, vinciri, verberari, ferroque necari patior*. Yet gladiators were extremely popular, and their images became common on statues, paintings, mosaics and graffiti.

Fighters entered a training school, *ludus*. Once taking the oath, the gladiator became a *tiro* until his first fight when he graduated to a *veteranus*. The training period lasted about six months and was overseen by a *lanista*. Julius Caesar's training school at Capua had 5,000 men. Domitian introduced the *Ludus Magnus* in Rome, built just east of the Colosseum to provide a ready supply of fighters. Three others quickly followed: *Ludus Dacicus*, *Ludus Gallicus* and *Ludus Matutinus*. Gladiatorial troupes were named after their owners, for example *Fustini familia gladiatoria*, named after a certain Faustus.

Some men could win their freedom or signed up for a set period of time. Those that were sentenced to *damnati ad ludum gladiatorium* or *damnati ad ludos* (as opposed to *damnati ad gladium*) had at least the chance of winning the wooden sword, *rudis*, the sign of their release from the *sacramentum gladiatorium*. However, those under *damnati ad gladium*, whilst they might survive a fight or two, were fated to die within a set period, likely no more than a year.[35]

Vegetius in the fourth century provided some details about the training. The recruits were provided with wooden swords and shields made from woven withies. Both were double the weight of normal swords and shields. They trained in the morning and afternoon against six-feet-high wooden posts sunk into the ground. The recruit attacked the post aiming for the head, flanks and hamstrings, all the time ensuring he did not expose himself to any potential counter blow. They learned to strike with the point and not the edge, as the edge seldom kills whereas a thrust of two inches can be fatal.

Archaeological evidence supports the literary sources in their dietary habits. Pliny the Elder claimed that gladiators were once known as *hordearii*, or barley-men, possibly due to a common dish of *sagina*, barley stew. It would seem they ate very little meat and added beans and dried fruit to their diet. The fact that some willingly volunteered to enter a gladiatorial school and give up their rights would suggest that either it wasn't as dangerous as it would appear or that the rewards outweighed any risk. How dangerous exactly was the life of a gladiator?

Life expectancy

Literary and epigraphical sources provide just enough evidence to piece together clues relating to the life expectancy of a gladiator.[36] On average, a new fighter entered the arena at 17, fought approximately eight fights and was expected to live five-and-a-half years. That equates to just two fights a year. As such it is more like the experience of a modern professional boxer rather than the free-for-all deadly mass-brawls depicted in some films and TV shows. One would expect more fights early in a career with a highly valued famous fighter risked only for a big occasion. However, there were occasions when gladiators fought multiple times in the same games, one example stating that a second fight was seven days after the first. At the extreme end, some fighters notched up fifty fights in their careers and were able to die of old age in their beds.

Other examples describe a man aged 22 who survived thirteen bouts and another aged 35 with twenty wins.[37] One famous inscription dated to the second century describes the career of a Syrian, Flamma, who fought as a *secutor*. *Flamma secutor vixit annos XXX pugnavit XXXIIII vicit XXI stans VIIII missus IIII natione Syrus huic Delicatus coarmio merenti fecit*. This translates as: 'Flamma, Secutor. He lived 30 years and fought 34 times, winning 21 bouts, drawing 9, and was spared 4 times. Syrian by birth. Delicatus, his comrade, made this for a worthy man'.

Other examples exist from inscriptions: Glauco died at 23 in his eighth fight; a second, aged 27 with eleven fights; and a third aged 34 with twenty-one contests. Glauco's inscription reads as follows (CIL 5.3466): 'To the revered spirits of the dead. Glauco, born at Mutino, fought seven times, died in the eighth. He lived 23 years, 5 days. Aurelia set this up to her well-deserving husband, together with those who loved him ... .'

In contrast, the average life expectancy for Roman males was 31, although the high rate of infant mortality skews this. If one reached the age of 17, then the average age of death rose to 48. Thus, the life of a gladiator certainly was dangerous and reduced life expectancy. The question is: how dangerous? One historian estimates the chance of being killed at nine-to-one.[38] This reduced to four-to-one if he lost his bout. Still hazardous, but we can see that the majority of fighters left the arena with their lives, even if they lost.

At one example in Pompeii the games consisted of twenty-three bouts with forty-six gladiators. Twenty-one were victorious, suggesting two were draws. Seventeen of the losers survived, while eight gladiators were killed or died from their wounds. This suggests that one or two of the winners succumbed to injuries, too. Eight out of forty-six gives a percentage of seventeen, or just under one in six.

At the beginning of the imperial period Augustus reformed the *munera*. Fights to the death, *sine missione*, were prohibited. This did not last and by the time of Vespasian the mob once more screamed for the life or death of a fallen fighter. In Campania, over four days, out of eleven pairs of gladiators eleven fighters were killed, along with ten bears. Approximately three quarters died before their tenth fight. From these examples we can estimate an attrition rate of one-in-six to one-in-eight. In percentage terms this is roughly 13–16 per cent.

Sometimes both fighters fell. A certain Decoratus, a *secutor*, veteran of nine fights, killed a *retiarius* called Caeruleus but then fell dead. We read 'the trainer's rod killed them both' but we are not told why or how. Some epigraphs claim foul play: Diodorus claims to have defeated Demetrius but did not kill him immediately. Perhaps he had him at his mercy but was forced to step back as we read 'murderous fate and the cunning treachery of the *summa rudis* killed me'. Another tells us that Pardo of Dertona, a veteran of ten fights, was somehow 'deceived in the eleventh', an epigraphical version of 'we was robbed', familiar to many a football fan.

Winning didn't guarantee survival either. A certain Batavian called Vitalis, an unbeaten *retiarius*, fought it out to the end on an equal footing with his opponent. The text breaks off after his friend Himen recalls Vitalis 'was fast in his fights'. Did he succumb to his wounds in a fight? We get a vivid picture of the sort of injuries inflicted from Galen, the physician to Emperor Marcus Aurelius. He started his career treating gladiators in Pergamum, modern Turkey, and one example given is of his replacing intestines hanging out of a gaping wound.

Given these dangers, it is perhaps surprising that some free-born men volunteered. Most fighters were forced: prisoners, slaves or criminals. Some prisoners were so terrified of the ordeal that they committed suicide rather than fight.[39] Seneca recalls a gruesome incident involving a Germanic animal hunter trying to avoid the arena. Perhaps he was a lowly *bestiarii* and was aware of what awaited him. Whatever the context it was a desperate decision. When he went to relieve himself, he took the stick with a sponge on the end used by the Romans as a version of lavatory paper. He then proceeded to ram it down his own throat and choked to death. In the late empire twenty-nine captured Saxons strangled each other rather than be forced to fight.

Violence wasn't only confined to the arena floor either. Nor was it only the well-documented riots often caused by supporters of different chariot teams. Seneca records that scuffles often broke out as spectators fought over items thrown into the crowd. Such prizes could be sweets or breads but also tokens that could be redeemed for more expensive items. In the early third century, under the Emperor Elagabulus, this caused a number of deaths. In AD 59 major crowd violence erupted at a *munus* in Pompeii.[40] A number of spectators attended from the neighbouring town of Nuccria and town rivalry caused insults to be exchanged. This escalated into violence and a significant number of spectators died. The subsequent inquiry banned Pompeii from holding games for ten years.

In summary, the life of a gladiator was not quite as dangerous as some might expect. It had a significant impact on life expectancy but some fighters lived to enjoy their retirement. The rewards were enough to lure young men to volunteer despite, or perhaps because of, the danger. At the same time the horrors were enough to drive others to suicide.

There was probably a range of experiences. A young man seeking fame and glory might eagerly await his matched-pair, confident in his skill. At the same time a condemned man, knowing he was doomed to die if not on this day but at some point in the coming months, would have no cause for any optimism. We can only wonder how those condemned to face wild beasts felt as they entered the arena floor, unarmed and unarmoured.

One of the drivers preventing all defeated gladiators from being automatically killed was the cost. Aside from the initial outlay, a considerable amount of time and effort went in to training these men.

Costs

We can estimate the total numbers of gladiators across the empire and associated costs.[41] To put things into perspective, a peasant family could live on as little as 500 sesterces a year whereas the pay of a legionary soldier was about 225 denarii, or 900 sesterces. A skilled fighter cost between 3,000 and 15,000 sesterces, between over three to fifteen years' annual pay of a soldier. A senior gladiator was called a *primus palus*, similar to the *primus pilus*, senior centurion of the first century in a legion. Other entertainers and workers in the arena were priced at 1,000 to 2,000 sesterces, similar to an unskilled slave.

By the end of the second century there were four grades of *munera*, and the following figures are based on four sesterces being an average day's pay and equivalent to £25-30.[42] The lowest, class IV, costing between 30-60,000 (£200-£400,000) and the highest, class I, costing between 150-200,000 (£1-£1.25 million). For many emperors the cost was not a barrier with Hadrian once spending 2 million sesterces (£12.5 million). This values the gladiators at between £22,500 to £112,500. Perhaps a better comparison would be using average earnings of a modern UK full-time worker, £38,131. A Roman worker might earn approximately 1,000 sesterces a year. Thus a gladiator cost three to fifteen times an average worker's annual wage. The modern equivalent would value these elite fighters at between nearly £115,000 to £572,000, a bargain when compared to many modern top-flight footballers.

The highest paid gladiators cost the equivalent of nearly a year's wages for a full century in a Roman cohort. In addition, a sizeable amount of time and effort went into their training. Replacing those men was not an insignificant logistical problem. There were over 200 stone amphitheatres throughout the empire and the estimate of total arenas is around double that. On average, only around five days of the year might have been used for gladiatorial contests with the rest used for less bloodthirsty shows and entertainment. From this we can make some rough estimates of attrition rates.

The total number of gladiators may have been around 12,000, fighting in two shows per year, thus 24,000 individual appearances. With a death rate of one in eight, 3,000 would need replacing each year. Pliny claims that under Caligula there were 20,000 gladiators in training camps, equivalent to nearly four legions. It is difficult to be precise but if we take the higher figure this would equate to 5,000 deaths per year (1/8 of 2 x 20,000). A legion-sized force required recruiting and training every year.

It required a steady stream of slaves and criminals alongside a much smaller number of volunteers eager for fame or glory. Vespasian and Titus had a ready supply of Jewish prisoners. Many of these were put to work, with a substantial number on the Colosseum. A significant number would meet their ends in similar arenas across the empire. We get very few contemporary accounts but, fortunately, one that survives comes during the reign of Titus.

Contemporary accounts

Very few contemporary accounts survive to give an accurate picture of a gladiator bout. However, one fight from the Flavian period stands out.[43] Priscus and Verus fought a long battle that ended in a draw. Their names, meaning 'ancient' and 'true' respectively, were likely stage names. The rules meant the fight only stopped when one fighter was either killed or conceded. It was up to the sponsor of the show, the *editor*, to decide if the defeated gladiator was to be killed. This was often the emperor, but a wise man listened carefully to the crowd. The Latin phrase *pollice verso* means 'thumbs turned', but we don't know what exactly this means or which way the thumbs pointed for life or death.

Martial described the fight:[44] Priscus 'dragged out to the right' and Verus mirrored his movements. The battle went on for a long time and the crowd repeatedly roared for both men to be discharged from the arena. Neither man would yield and the exhausted pair fought to a stalemate. Titus kept to the rules which, Martial tells us, meant once the contest had started it ran on until *ad digitum*, 'to the finger'. Eventually the exhausted pair surrendered together. The text suggests this was perhaps imposed upon them as Martial states, 'At long last a way to end this perfectly matched contest was hit upon'. Caesar sent gifts and palms to each of them to mark their joint victory. The crowd demanded an 'honourable discharge' from gladiatorial service and Titus accordingly sent both men the wooden sword symbolising their freedom.

A tombstone at Trieste was provided by a certain Constantius who was responsible for the *munus*: 'To Decorates the *retiarius*, who killed Caeruleus and died himself, as both died by the same sword, so the same pyre covers both. Decorates, the *secutor*, after nine fights left his wife Valeria grieving for the first time.'[45] It would appear the winner of the fight himself later succumbed to his wounds.

From Pompeii graffiti shows two fighters: A *tiro*, novice, Marcus Attilius and Hilarus, victor in twelve out of fourteen fights.[46] No doubt gambling money fell heavily on the experienced fighter and, if so, they would have been sorely disappointed. The novice won whilst his rival was 'sent away', meaning, although defeated, he lived to fight another day.

It was traditional for gladiators to have their last meal in public.[47] Perhaps Priscus and Verus supped together with the other matched pairs the evening before the fight. The gladiatorial display was the high point of games. Spectators could come and view the fighters the night or morning before the fight. The fighters could be inspected as one might look at a thoroughbred horse before a race.

To see why the gladiators became so popular we can turn to an excerpt from *The Confessions* of St Augustine of Hippo, written at the end of the fourth century. A young man called Alypius arrived in Rome with a deep aversion and distaste of such spectacles. He was persuaded to go by his friends and was reluctantly dragged to the arena. As a devout young Christian, he was determined to shut his eyes to what he viewed as an evil and wicked display. Perhaps he was ready to be seduced when he saw for the first time the Colosseum rising four storeys high. Or perhaps it was the sight of the arena floor after he walked under the arches, up the steps and to his seat. The expanse of yellow sand might have had the same effect on him as the first visit to a football stadium has on a young football fan today. That first sight of bright green spread out like a carpet, ready for the contest to come.

For Alypius the final straw was the roar of the crowd. So vehement and loud, he was overcome by curiosity. Maybe he really did have his eyes closed or covered by his hands. If so, he must have tentatively looked through his fingers. Then he removed his hands and took a better look. A fighter fell to the floor and the crowd erupted. Swept up in the atmosphere, Alyprius soon found himself enjoying it. Even eager for more. He began shouting with his friends. By the end of the bouts, he was as enthusiastic as any of them delighted by the 'murderous contest and was inebriated by bloodthirsty pleasure'. No longer the timid, quiet, peaceloving Christian he had been when he came in, he was one of the crowd, on fire with emotion. He was hooked and took what Augustine describes as the 'madness' home with him. From that moment he became obsessed with gladiatorial spectacles, no doubt to the deep disappointment of Augustine.

Mock battles

Individual contests were not the only entertainment. Several examples of mock battles exist. In 29 BC Dacian and Suevi prisoners fought a large-scale engagement in Rome.[48] On this occasion a Roman senator, Quintus Vitellius, was able to take part despite the earlier ban by Augustus. Both Julius Caesar and Claudius had put on mass combat displays.[49] It was noted earlier how Claudius watched a mock battle scene replicating an assault on a British settlement. This probably represented Camulodunum, an event Claudius no doubt took full credit for despite only being in Britain for sixteen days. It would have been a simple matter for Vespasian to represent one of his great victories against the Britons in his westward campaign. The emperor Hadrian had 300 condemned criminals fight, some wearing distinctive gold cloaks.[50]

The film *Gladiator* has a mock-battle scene in the Colosseum, supposedly portraying the Battle of Zama in 202 BC. The hero, Maximus Decimus Meridius, appears in the Colosseum for the first time. He leads a small number of mail-clad gladiators armed with shields and spears. A Roman audience, expecting the famous battle with infantry, cavalry and elephants, might have been surprised to see six scythed chariots, each pulled by two horses, enter the arena.

Some elements of the scene are not unlikely. Firstly, each chariot had a driver and a woman fighter wearing gold-coloured armour who peppered the infantry with arrows and javelins. Augustus had banned women competing in 22 BC which implies they did indeed take part in games. In fact, it may have been the sight of a woman of 'noble rank' participating along with equestrians that caused Augustus to legislate against both.[51] Vespasian's son Domitian staged events involving women and dwarves, albeit likely for comedic value.[52] Yet not long after, the poet Juvenal is horrified that some women fought as gladiators. Martial tells of a female hunter who rivals Hercules: 'We have now seen such things done by women's valour.'[53] It would appear that professional female fighters did compete in games during the second century. The practice was common enough for Septimius Severus to again ban female gladiators during his reign (AD 193–211).

It is not the presence of female gladiators or chariots that might cause historians to raise an eyebrow. Rather it is that the Romans were quite capable of putting on a reasonably accurate portrayal. For the battle of Zama that meant elephants. There are multiple accounts of elephants taking part in games such as when Pompey staged an event at the Circus Maximus.[54] To look at how the Romans might have re-enacted the scene in reality we need to turn to the battle which took place in modern Tunisia in 202 BC.

The battle marked the end of the Second Punic War between Rome and Carthage. Nearly two decades before Rome had been on the back foot. The war began in 219 BC when Hannibal besieged and sacked the pro-Roman city of Saguntum in eastern Spain. Rome declared war and the following year Hannibal famously crossed the Alps with his elephants and invaded northern Italy.

Several famous victories followed: Trebia, 218 BC, Lake Trasimene 217 BC and Cannae in 216 BC, where Hannibal was able to surround a much larger army and destroy it, killing 80,000 Romans. Some Italian cities, Syracuse and Macedonia, joined the Carthaginians. The war dragged on and Hannibal was unable to capitalise on his victories by capturing Rome. The tide turned with the rise of the Roman general Publius Scipio, first defeating Hannibal's brother, Hasdrubal Barca, in Iberia by 206 BC, then by invading North Africa in 204 BC. Hannibal was forced to return from Italy, setting up the climactic battle.

On the plains of Zama, 29,000 Roman infantry and 6,000 cavalry faced 36,000 Carthaginians with 4,000 cavalry. Hannibal had eighty elephants which he hoped would prove crucial. Both armies formed up in three lines flanked by cavalry. The battle began when Hannibal ordered his elephants forward with light skirmishers.

The Romans had learnt their lessons well. The cavalry blew horns and made enough noise to frighten half the elephants to turn in terror. The Carthaginian elephants smashed through their own left flank, causing their skirmishers and cavalry to scatter. The Roman cavalry saw an opportunity and took it, driving off the Carthaginian cavalry on both flanks. Meanwhile, the remaining elephants were lured on by light javelin-men. Formed up in lines rather than the traditional checker-board formation, the elephants avoided the massed ranks and plunged into the gaps. There they were met with a wall of spears and despatched with missile weapons.

The Roman infantry pushed forward and engaged the Carthaginian first line. The second and third lines soon joined the battle which went back and forth for some time. The pivotal moment was the return of the victorious Roman cavalry. This was a reversal of Hannibal's victory at Cannae. They slammed into the rear of Hannibal's force. Hannibal's army wavered, then broke. The retreat turned into a rout. Carthage lost half of its army. How then might the Romans have portrayed this battle?

There would be no need to display eighty elephants or even to kill one. The logistics of removing an elephant carcass speedily might prove too much. Far simpler to have two opposing infantry lines facing each other. Two or three elephants being driven through gaps in the line and then out of the arena through the 'gate of death' would be enough to replicate what happened. The two lines of fighters could then engage. Perhaps the *editor* ensured the team representing the Romans had the advantage. Easily done with numbers or quality of fighters. A hundred prisoners with little training would stand little chance against a similar number of experienced gladiators. Yet one wouldn't want too quick a victory. The crowd would be eager for a grand finale which would involve cavalry entering the arena and attacking from the rear.

How then might Vespasian display one of his great victories in Britain? A raised area in the centre of the arena could represent an *oppidum*, perhaps Maiden Castle. The 'Britons' would have to look the part. Just as Caligula disguised some prisoners as Germans, an editor of a show might strip his prisoners to the waist and paint bright blue patterns across their faces and torsos. Armed with large swords, spears and shields, they awaited their fate behind a makeshift palisade.

At the sound of horns, the crowd would cheer as a column of Roman legionaries marched into the arena. The crowd wanted blood but they also wanted entertainment. No time for a long siege here. Instead, they would attack using *testudo* formation. The doomed defenders would throw everything they had at their attackers but all their missiles simply bounced off the curved shields. Finally, up against the palisade, the rear ranks knelt and the formation formed a ramp with their shields.

Now comes the entertainment. The attackers run up the shields and over the top of their comrades to the battlements. In threes and fours, they jump down into the defenders. Of course, this would either be carefully choreographed or fixed so that the attackers had an advantage. One wouldn't want to be responsible for losing a famous battle in front of the emperor, especially if it was one of Vespasian's own victories. The crowd would cheer with each group of assailants as they made their charge. Modern football crowds hoot and holler as goalkeepers prepare to take a goal kick. We can imagine a similar noise as a legionary ran up the shield-ramp and jumped into the fray. Perhaps they attacked from all four sides at once, giving all sides of the arena a fantastic view.

Naumachia, naval battles

Whilst logistically more difficult, the Romans also put on elaborate displays on water. Some amphitheatres could hold a body of water and drain it afterwards. Nero used the Campus Martius for one such event in AD 57. He built a new amphitheatre on the site and flooded the arena in order to stage a mock naval battle from history involving the Athenians and Persians. Fish and marine animals were added for effect. Once ended, the water was drained away and a mock land battle ensued between the same groups. This was followed by a battle involving hundreds including senators and equestrians Nero had compelled to fight. One part of the show involved seeing aquatic animals in their natural habitat, seals and hippopotamus among them.

Julius Caesar put on a number of such displays, such as in 46 BC involving 2,000 oarsmen and 1,000 warriors. Often such displays were held on artificial lakes. In 2 BC Augustus recreated the battle of Salamis, 480 BC, fought between the Greeks and the Persians. Thirty *triremes* and *biremes* were manned by 3,000 gladiators and likely many more oarsmen and sailors fought against each other. Over two days, a similar mock battle saw 'Athenian' marines winning an initial naval engagement before storming an artificial island and capturing a fortress.

Emperor Claudius presented one of the most extravagant examples of a *numachia* in AD 52. It was held at Faucine, a natural lake just outside Rome. A mock battle between Sicilians and Rhodians involved 19,000 prisoners. A raft and breastworks surrounded the lake. Manning this perimeter was the Praetorian Guard, one of their tasks, no doubt, to deter 'deserters'. The other task was to use ballistae and catapults to fire missiles at any ships not performing as expected. The lake was large enough to allow the ships to manoeuvre and use their battering rams.

It is here we find the only reference to the famous line often assumed to be spoken by gladiators. The prisoners reportedly said '*ave Caesar, morituri the salutant*', which means, 'Hail Caesar. Those who about to die salute you.' There is no record of this being repeated in any other context and certainly not at individual gladiatorial contests at the Colosseum or anywhere else.[55]

Domitian staged a series of games to celebrate his victories against the Dacians. One of the events involved a *numachia* held in a new location Domitian had excavated for the purpose.[56] Suetonius implies a *numachia* was also held in the Colosseum which suggests it may not have been wholly suitable if Domitian was forced to hold one at a different location. It is possible alterations to the basement made the use of water impractical. The addition of animal cages, ramps and pulleys could make drainage difficult. Cassius Dio records that Titus filled the arena with water and brought in animals to swim for the crowds, followed by a mock naval battle.

Despite this, there remains a debate about whether the Colosseum was able to be flooded.[57] The infrastructure and logistics seem inadequate, yet the sources suggest it did happen. The staging of *naumachia* seems to have declined as Elagabalus, 218-222, was one of the first emperors for some time to stage one. The last recorded *naumachia* was in the year 274 under the Emperor Aurelian.

If Vespasian or Titus wanted to commemorate a battle involving water, then the most likely examples from Vespasian's career would be one of the river crossings in the campaign in Britain in 43. It would be an easy task to construct a river across the arena floor, either by digging out a small trench or lining a shallow wooden construction a few feet wide. The crowd wouldn't much care if it didn't reflect accurately the width and depth of the Medway or Thames.

What they wanted to see was blood. Who better to use as Britons than prisoners and criminals, badly armed and poorly armoured. Trumpets would sound and those playing the parts of Germanic auxiliaries could cross the river first. The crowd would cheer even louder as Roman legionaries advanced across a man-made 'ford'. Fantastic entertainment before the main event: the gladiator pairs.

Single combat

After the epic Battle of Zama scene in *Gladiator*, Maximus is matched against Tigris the Gaul. Whilst it is thoroughly entertaining, we have seen that the weapons and armour in the film are far from being accurate. Earlier scenes with Maximus fighting multiple opponents singlehandedly, all wearing a variety exotic armour and helmets, are equally unrealistic. Into this fight tigers are introduced.

Tigers were a novelty when Augustus exhibited one in 11 BC.[58] They were more common by the time of Marcus Aurelius, though far more expensive than the usual lions and bears. Such beasts were used against criminals and beast hunters. There isn't much evidence that they fought against gladiators. Gladiators were expensive to train and a valuable asset.

Gladiator bouts were designed to match two finely balanced fighters. Such as the lightly-armed *retiarius* against the heavily-armed *secutor*. The crowd wanted to see two evenly matched fighters, such as *provocators* armed with *scutum* and gladius, or a *hoplomachus* spearman against a *thraex* with short curved sword. Alternatively, a heavily-protected *myrhillo* with sword and *scutum* shield.

Earlier we met Priscus and Verus, who fought to an exhausted draw before the emperor. Despite the dearth of contemporary accounts, we can get some idea from re-enactments. In one example, a *retiarius* faces up to a *secutor*. The retiarius is the taller of the two, armed with a three-pronged *fuscina*, or trident but no helmet, shield or greaves. His only clothing is short trousers with a broad belt around his waist. His only armour a *manica* on his left arm and a large *galerus* protecting his left shoulder, neck and head. He held the bottom of the trident and weighted net in his right hand with his left about two-thirds up the shaft of the spear.

Facing him was a *secutor*, shorter and stockier than his opponent and protected by a large *scutum* shield. Taking a boxer's stance, he wore a greave on his forward left leg. In his right arm, which was heavily protected by a *manica*, he held a gladius. His helmet had a visor which covered his face and a fish adorned the large crest. Facing him, one would be unable to see any bare flesh. To get a strike on target required getting around or inside his defences, or waiting for him to tire and drop his guard just enough.

Between the two men stood the *summa rudis*. Only on his signal did the fight begin. The *retiarius* probed first, easily deflected by the large shield. The *secutor* countered with the gladius but the reach was too short. Three times this probing and counter-thrust occurred before the *secutor* moved in to close the gap. The *retiarius* deployed his net but it sailed harmlessly over his opponent's helmet. For a moment the trident kept the *secutor* at bay, but he moved forward quickly. Using his shield to good effect for a split second he was inside the tip of the trident.

The fight could have easily ended at that point but the *retiarius* retreated quickly and skipped away some distance. He wheeled to the right and then came in holding his weapon two-handed. Two quick thrusts contacted with the shield and then helmet. Still the *secutor* came on. The *retiarius* tried to hook his discarded net with his trident but his opponent stepped in and attacked using the edge of his shield. The now net-less man retreated again.

The *secutor* then made the move that decided the bout. He moved in quickly and used his shield to knock the trident to his left. The *retiarius* had no room to swing his weapon round and could not retreat quickly enough to a defensive position. The more heavily armoured fighter bulldozed his opponent backwards until he was close enough to thrust at exposed skin. In this case it was the left shoulder blade just below the *galerus*, the large metal plate protecting the shoulder.

The whole fight lasted less than two minutes and ended with this first hit. In this case, of course, it caused no injury. A strike with a real gladius would have cut deep. In reality, a Roman *retiarius* might well fight on, especially if one feared angering the crowd or *editor* with an early submission. Some fights may have lasted mere seconds if an initial attack was immediately successful. Most probably lasted less than a round or two of a modern boxing match. Perhaps some were choreographed for entertainment value. Whatever the case, gladiators became the celebrities and sports stars of the Roman world. The games were an integral part of Roman culture. Vespasian's contribution to that still stands today in Rome.

Summary

The Colosseum is perhaps one of Vespasian's greatest legacies. The remains of it still stand as testament to Roman engineering prowess nearly 2,000 years after its construction. The spectacles organised within its walls evolved over many centuries. Beginning as part of funeral ceremonies, gladiators become an integral part of Roman society. The games themselves became an elaborate display of Roman power and culture.

By the time of Vespasian, emperors would project their power and largesse through ever more extravagant spectacles. A typical games might last several days and begin with beast hunts and animal shows. The latter might be little more than modern circus acts. By mid-morning one could be entertained by a criminal being despatched by a bear or lion in a re-enactment of some horrific Greek myth. For a modern fainthearted observer worse was to come. But the average Roman would have happily had his lunch and cheered as criminals and prisoners were burnt, crucified and torn apart by lions and bears.

Vespasian was not a great fan of such spectacles, unlike some of his predecessors and successors. It is interesting to compare him to Caligula, Claudius and Nero on this point. They were all keen fans of such contests. Yet none had the battlefield experience of Vespasian. The new emperor had seen enough blood. Yet his position would force him to attend and play his part. An afternoon's mock battle might show one of his great victories in Britain or Judea. What might a battle-hardened Vespasian feel when watching fighters dressed as legionnaires butchering prisoners playing the part of Britons or Jews?

Chapter 7

EMPEROR

Back in late December 69 the Colosseum was still a glint in Vespasian's eye. To the victor the spoils. Vespasian had been declared emperor on the 21st, the day after Vitellius had been mercilessly cut down on the Gemonian stairs. Titus and Domitian, 29 and 18 years old respectively, shared in their father's success, each being titled Caesar. Within Rome there was little enthusiasm among the plebs for the new emperor. They had in turn all cheered, and later jeered, for Nero, Galba, Otho and Vitellius. What people needed was safety, food and peace. Vespasian offered stability.

Cassius Dio tells us that 'portents and dreams had come to Vespasian pointing to the sovereignty long beforehand'. An ox was said to have approached and knelt before him, placing its head beneath its feet. A tree, uprooted by a storm, was found upright the following day. The words of Josephus are quoted: 'You may imprison me now, but a year from now, when you have become emperor, you will release me.' There had been a prophecy that a future ruler would emerge from the east. This was useful to some Jewish leaders as it gave legitimacy to, and justification for, their surrender to the Romans. In similar vein, he was hailed in Alexandria as 'son of Ammon' and thus legitimate 'King of Egypt', favoured by and linked to Serapis, the Greco-Egyptian Sun god.

Vespasian had also acquired a curious reputation for being able to cure people.[1] Whilst still in Egypt he was approached by a blind man and another with a crippled limb requesting a cure. Asked to apply spittle to the first man's eyes and place his foot on the second man's limb he was initially sceptical. Encouraged by his physicians and advisors he did so. Those examples, and the prophecies above, all might have been a cynical cultivation of local myths. Perhaps Vespasian himself was duped by manipulative local elites set on ingratiating themselves with the new regime.

However, with the coming of a new year nothing was certain. There was no guarantee that further usurpers would not raise their heads. The Batavian and Judean revolts were still to be quashed. Vespasian never lost sight of who he had to thank for his position. Whilst he imposed a harsher discipline on the troops, unlike Vitellius he ensured that a donative was paid. He dated his accession not from the senate's proclamation on 21 December but from 1 July when the troops had acclaimed him. He allowed the troops to salute him as Imperator no fewer than twenty times.

When Vespasian finally returned to Rome, Suetonius claims his priority was to bring 'order to the empire, ravaged and collapsing as it was'. Provinces and cities were brought back under control. The Capitol, scarred by fire and war, was rebuilt. Suetonius even claims Vespasian personally got his hands dirty, assisting in removing rubble, 'some of which he carried away on his own back'. A shrewd political move perhaps.

Copies of bronze tablets destroyed in the temple fire, 'most ancient and precious records', were hunted down and replaced. He also instigated new building works: the Temple of Peace next to the Forum; Temple of the Deified Claudius on the Caelian Hill; and the Amphitheatre.

The senatorial and equestrian orders, which had been 'reduced … and debased' by the civil wars, were 'purged and reinforced'. Unworthy members were expelled and Vespasian brought in many from the provinces. He emphasised the distinction between the two orders by position rather than privileges. Vespasian also addressed social matters. If a freewoman had a relationship with someone else's slave, she was considered a slave-woman. Presumably sleeping with one's own slave was permissible. Militarily, he raised the status of auxiliary units by allowing Roman citizens to join.[2] It is thought he re-organised the praetorians in Rome, reducing the number of cohorts from sixteen to nine.

Tacitus argues that conferring supreme power in the hands of a single man was in the interest of peace. Vespasian was indeed viewed by contemporary and later historians as a stabilising influence. There were no examples of the gratuitous violence that other emperors engaged in, such as Caligula or Nero. Later emperors such as Commodus and Caracalla were to prove even more murderous. Instead, the Flavian dynasty, despite the rule of Domitian, heralded a period known as 'The Five Good Emperors'. These included Nerva (96-98), Trajan (98-117),

Hadrian (117-138, Antoninus Pius (138-161) and Marcus Aurelius (161-180). Cassius Dio famously stated that the transfer of power from Marcus Aurelius to his son Commodus saw the empire lurch from a 'Kingdom of Gold to one of iron and rust'.

Vespasian is described by Suetonius as patient, tolerant, unassuming and lenient. He 'bore not the slightest grudge against those who insulted or opposed him'. A number of examples are given where he replied with humour even when insulted to his face. Nero or Caligula would have responded very differently. In some ways, he styled himself on Augustus, giving an outward display of respecting the senate. In practice, he increased imperial control. In 73-4 he occupied the position of *censor* allowing him control over membership of the senate.

Back in early 70 with the civil war over, Vespasian's three major problems were dealt with methodically. The first was to secure and stabilise his position. Primus had entered Rome, at the head of the Flavian army, the day after Vitellius's murder. The smoke from the remains of the Temple of Jupiter still hung in the air. Mucianus arrived not long after and criticised Primus for committing atrocities. Primus headed east to complain directly to the new emperor and was pacified with honours. It was Mucianus, though, who wielded power in Rome throughout much of the first year of Vespasian's reign. Vitellius's son was among several potential rivals executed. Vespasian could legitimately claim to have clean hands, but Mucianus was to remain a loyal advisor until his death c. 76.

The second problem was the war in Judea, the third the Batavian revolt on the Rhine. In April of Vespasian's first year as emperor his son Titus laid siege to Jerusalem. Two months later the Batavians were defeated outside Castra Vetera. By the end of August the Temple in Jerusalem and the Batavian capital at Nijmegen had been destroyed. The Batavians could hold out no longer and, knowing troops could now be diverted from the east, sued for peace and renewed their alliance. The Judean war was to drag on. Whilst the temple was burned in August the city itself held out for another month. To the south Masada held on for three more years but the war was effectively over.

The army was re-organised. The legions that had supported Vitellius were moved away from key positions. The large camps of the Rhine and Danube were broken up. No longer were two legions allowed to billet together. One of their complaints had been that Vitellius intended to move them away from areas in which they had ties. Vespasian wisely allowed them to remain, and legions become more static. Auxiliary units were a different matter. They now tended to be based away from their homelands. In addition, he drafted a variety of ethnicities into units so that they lost some of their individual ethnic identity.

It wasn't until October 70 that Vespasian finally entered Rome. By then the situation across the empire was largely stable but Jerusalem had finally fallen the month before to Titus. One thing the Roman mob loved almost as much as gladiatorial contests was a Triumph. Vespasian was canny enough to seize the opportunity even though, in Judea, Masada desperately held on. Before we look at the Triumphal procession of Vespasian and Titus, let us briefly turn to the siege of Jerusalem.

Siege of Jerusalem

Vespasian's campaign through Galilee and Judea had been paused in late 68 as he awaited orders from the new emperor Galba. Tacitus stated that the 'whole of the level country' and all the cities had been subdued. All, of course, except Jerusalem. As for the mountainous regions, Masada was to prove the most stubborn. With news of Galba's assassination and Otho's ascension in January of the following year, together with Vitellius's march on Rome, the empire held its breath. News of the battle of Bedriacum and Otho's demise came in April. The subsequent continuation of the civil war and the Flavians' eventual victory allowed Jerusalem a few months before the inevitable storm hit its walls.

The city of Jerusalem was built on rising ground incorporating two hills within its walls. Towers were sixty-feet high and in places even double that. An inner wall surrounded the palace. The Temple itself was 'built like a citadel'. Three main groups defended the city, whose population had been swollen by refugees and pilgrims. A force of approximately 15,000 led by Simon held the outer wall and the Old Town. John led a smaller force of 6,000 in the New Town in the middle of the city. The Temple was held by 2,400 zealots led by Eleazar. Tacitus tells us that these three groups were constantly fighting among themselves. Eventually, John gained dominance over the Temple, leaving two main groups defending the city. To the north was a fourth quarter called Bezetha which contained the bulk of the pilgrims. Tacitus puts the number in the city at 600,000.

On 14 April 70, during Passover, Titus besieged the city. To the north-east two legions set up camp, *Legio XII Fulminata* and *Legio XV Apollinaris*. A short distance away was *Legio V Macedonica*. A fourth legion, *Legio X Fretensis*, occupied the Mount of Olives, facing the Temple. Accompanying them were auxiliaries from client kings and veterans of the defeated armies of Otho and Galba.

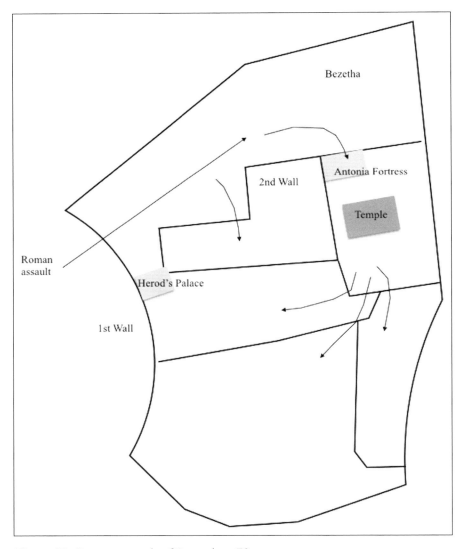

Figure 59: Roman assault of Jerusalem 70.

The Romans began the attack with artillery and battering rams. Attempted sorties by the defenders to destroy the siege engines failed and, within fifteen days, the outer wall fell. Five days later, the second wall was breached and Romans poured into the New Town. After four days of heavy fighting and considerable losses the Romans withdrew.

The assault was renewed and after another four days of vicious conflict the Romans managed to destroy much of a section of the second wall. An attempt was made by Josephus, now working for Titus, to persuade the defenders to surrender. This was rebuffed and the Romans attempted to build siege ramps aimed at the Antonia fortress. All four were destroyed by the defenders through fire or undermining. The Romans decided to starve them out. Trees within a fifteen-kilometre radius were cut down and an eight-kilometre palisade constructed to surround the city.

It took until the beginning of July to finally take the Antonia fortress, causing the defenders to flee to the nearby Temple complex. The fort was demolished and the stones used to build a ramp against the Temple. By early September the Temple was ablaze, likely ordered by Titus although Josephus absolves his patron of the crime. What wasn't burned by fire was destroyed or taken. The Romans turned their attention to the Old Town and the survivors fled to the sewers. By 8 September they had surrendered and Titus was master of Jerusalem.

Josephus gives perhaps exaggerated numbers of casualties: the number of those who perished during the whole siege was 'eleven hundred thousand'. Perhaps this reflects those killed in the entire war across Judea. The number placed in captivity was a more believable 97,000.

Triumph

When Titus eventually returned to Rome, a great triumph was held to honour the conquerors of Judea. Jospehus describes it in great detail.[3] Titus brought with him 700 prisoners, among them the leaders Simon and John. Those 700 were selected specifically for being 'eminently tall and handsome of body' so as to look all the better when paraded through the streets of Rome. The senate had actually granted two separate Triumphs. However, father and son 'reunited to the joy of the populous' decided to hold theirs together.

The great day arrived and the whole city turned out to watch, taking positions along the route, barely leaving space for the procession itself. Perhaps the nearest comparison is a victory parade by a winning sports team. In 2022, the population turned out in Buenos Aires to celebrate Argentina's World Cup win. The team bus could barely move through the crowds. Millions turned out, dozens were injured and the progress had to be cancelled before the end. Perhaps a quarter of the near 16,000,000 population crammed the streets.

Back in Vespasian's Rome a similar atmosphere of excitement and anticipation filled the air. This was a carnival, victory parade and street party all rolled into one. The night before the soldiers had marched out and taken up position near the Temple of Isis where the two heroes had spent the night.

The next morning Vespasian and Titus appeared before the adoring but fickle multitude. Both men were crowned with laurel and clothed in purple. They walked a short distance to the Octavian's Walks where the senate and senior members of the equestrian order waited for them. The emperors sat upon ivory chairs and received the acclamation of their soldiers. These were dressed, not in their mail or armour, but silken garments and crowned not with the customary soldiers' helmets but laurels.

Vespasian stood and called for silence. Pulling his cloak up over his head he offered prayers to the gods. Titus, too, performed these solemn rites before his father gave a short speech and sent the soldiery off to feast, all expenses paid by the emperor. The famously miserly Vespasian knew who to thank for his position. The emperors retired through the 'Gate of the Pomp', ate a little and offered sacrifices to the gods.

Now dressed in their 'triumphal garments', they set off through the city. Accompanying them was a 'multitude of the shows … variety of riches, or the rarities of nature … heaped on another'. A 'mighty quantity of silver, and gold, and ivory' flowed through the city like a river. Some were carried, others pulled on carts. Precious jewels, embroideries and crowns of gold, images of the gods, notable for their huge size and workmanship, wove their way through the cheering crowds. Animals, too, were present, their handlers as richly adorned in purple and gold as the rest. Even the captives were dressed finely, although the clothes concealed 'the deformity of their bodies'.

All this would have been entertaining enough, yet the pageant contained a surprise even for a Roman audience. Bearers struggled under the weight of huge floats, some up to four storeys in height, many with rich golden carpets and wrought gold and ivory fastened about them all. Those showed the war in all its horrific glory: a country laid waste; entire squadrons of enemies slain; great fortifications overthrown and ruined by machines; the victorious Romans pouring over walls; slaughter and finally the submission of the enemy.

Ruined cities, burning temples, all were displayed for the mob. Such was the workmanship in this carnival procession that Josephus claimed it was as though one had been present in the war. The dreadful siege of Jotapata, the final assault, the burning of the temple in Jerusalem, all was there in its full bloody shock and awe. Sitting atop some of the floats was the enemy commander of the city displayed, or at least that is how it was presented. Humiliation atop humiliation for the defeated people. The greatest attraction was perhaps the treasure from the Temple of Jerusalem.

Following on came the solders carrying the images of Victory, in front of their emperors. Vespasian and Titus rode in a chariot and were followed by Domitian riding a great horse. They finally came to the temple of Jupiter Capitolinus and there they waited for a message. Not from the gods, but a messenger travelling the short distance from the Forum. Ancient custom demanded news of the enemy general's death. Simon had been dragged through Rome to his fate, tormented by his captors along the route. A rope placed around his neck, he was strangled.

The deed done and the news brought to the temple, a great shout of joy went up. More sacrifices and prayers followed before Vespasian and his sons retired to the palace. The festivities were not quite finished. A lucky few joined the imperial family but 'for all the rest there were noble preparations made for feasting at home'. The festival day was not just for the great victory but also the ending of 'their civil miseries'. Perhaps most importantly, Josephus adds that it was for the hope of future prosperity and happiness.

The Triumph was not just a victory parade. It was a political statement. It marked the ending not just of 'foreign' wars, but civil strife too. No matter that Judea had actually been a Roman province, it was presented as though it were a new conquest. Vespasian and Titus showed an astuteness lacking in their predecessors. They literally gave the mob food and spectacle, bread and circuses. The message was clear. This is what Flavian rule looks like. Success, victory and stability.

If any would-be usurpers waited in the wings they held their tongues and waited. But Vespasian avoided the mistakes of his predecessors. There were no mass executions which created new resentments. After eighteen months of bloody civil war, peace and stability were to be valued. As the political and economic situation stabilised, the new emperor was able to expand the empire's boundaries in the very province where he had made his reputation nearly thirty years before.

Britain under the Flavians

Tacitus provides a good summary of Roman activity in Britain in his book *Agricola*. The first governor of Consular rank was Aulus Plautius, Vespasian's commanding officer in the invasion of 43. He was followed by Ostorius Scapula.

Britain was 'brought into the condition of a province'. A colony of veterans was introduced at Camulodunum. The client king Cogidumnus was given control over several tribal areas and was still 'a most faithful ally' at the time of writing. Didius Gallus consolidated the Roman conquests and pushed the borders further inland. The next governor, Veranius, died within the year. So, we come to Suetonius Paulinus whom we met previously giving a rousing speech to his troops before the final battle against Boudicca. Several tribes were subdued before he advanced on the island of Mona. Indeed, aside from the extreme west, much of modern Wales, Britain south of the Humber had seemingly been brought to heel. The response to the heavy-handed approach of Roman officials proved otherwise.

The subsequent near disaster of the Boudiccan revolt left the province needing significant reinforcements. Eight auxiliary units, 1,000 cavalry and 2,000 legionaries were sent from Germany. The Ninth Legion at Lincoln had been particularly hard hit, having suffered a major defeat at the start of the rebellion. It has been suggested that those troops were brought over after c. 61 by the future emperor Titus, who had been a military tribune in Germania.[4]

Paulinus appears to have conducted a policy of vengeance against any tribes that had joined the rebellion or even stayed neutral. There is evidence of destruction at several hillforts, including South Cadbury that may be dated to this period. It is possible that Titus found himself attacking the same hillfort his father had assaulted eighteen years before. An inquiry was held and the more belligerent Paulinus was quietly replaced by Petronius Turpilianus, a more lenient man than his predecessors. Accompanied by a likeminded procurator, Classicianus, they set about trying to win hearts and minds. Whatever the new policy it seems to have worked. The southern Britons remained subdued over the following years.

By the end of Nero's reign, Roman rule had extended roughly to a line between the Mersey and Humber. Just north of that were the Brigantes, perhaps the largest tribe, or confederation of tribes, in Britain. Their territory stretched all the way to the lowlands of modern Scotland. One of their centres of power was Stanwick, a 741-acre site protected by a series of impressive earthworks. Archaeological evidence suggests there were significant trade links with the empire. Yet the bulk of the population lived, not in large *oppida*, but in small villages and farms.

During the first years of the Roman invasion, the queen of the Brigantes, Catimandua, had maintained good relations with the Romans. She had handed over the British rebel leader, Caractacus in c. 51. Eighteen years later civil conflict, and marital strife, threatened the status quo. Catimandua's estranged husband, Venutius, led an anti-Roman faction, and began to get the upper hand. Any hope of a peace was probably lost when the queen took her former husband's armour-bearer as a lover. So grave was the situation the Romans were forced to intervene and rescue the queen.

The Romans moved north and chose a location for a new fortress. It appears they selected a site that was devoid of any previous native settlements.[5] However, there is evidence for Roman military activity before the construction of the fortress.[6] The region had a number of advantages:[7] it lay between two tribal areas, the Parisi in the East Riding of Yorkshire, and the Brigantes to the west and north; roads linked with Lincoln in the south and Tadcaster to the south-west; the River Ouse gave easy access to the Humber and the sea; it was well placed on a piece of high ground providing access through the marshy Vale of York and it was well-protected by the rivers Ouse and Foss.

The fort was laid out in the traditional 'playing-card' shape measuring approximately 1,600 by 1,360 Roman feet. A ditch and rampart, approximately nine-feet high and nineteen-feet wide, was strengthened by timbers and turf. Atop this earthwork, an eight-feet-wide timber walkway was protected by a timber palisade. Evidence exists for timber towers at various points and the four gates, one each side, would have also been of timber. This inauspicious fort at the edge of the Roman world would evolve into one of Britain's greatest cities, Eboracum, York. In the second year of Vespasian's reign, the Ninth Legion was ordered from Lincoln to their new legionary base at the new fort.

Vespasian turned to two loyal supporters who were to have a significant impact on extending Roman dominance in Britain. The first was Quintus Pettilius Cerialis whom we last met putting down the Batavian revolt in the first year of Vespasian's reign. He had led the relief column of the Ninth which was all but destroyed by Boudicca in 61. Cerialis had barely escaped with his life. His appointment perhaps lay with his close connection with the new emperor; it is thought he had been his son-in-law, married to his daughter Flavia Domitilla. Sadly, neither Flavia nor her mother were to live long enough to see Vespasian as emperor.

Accompanying Cerialis was Gnaeus Julius Agricola. Agricola was appointed legate of the Twentieth which had replaced the Fourteenth at Wroxeter. The Fourteenth had been re-deployed to the Balkans by Nero in c. 67. Vespasian restored Britain's garrison strength to four legions by sending *Legio II Adiutrix*. This legion had been formed in c. 69 from the Adriatic fleet based at Ravenna, but had deserted Vitellius for Vespasian, earning it the title *Pia Fidelis*, 'dutiful and loyal'. It was to remain in Britain for fifteen years.

The legions based in Britain can be seen in the Table 6 below. Two legions, the Second Augusta and Twentieth, remained in Britain throughout the Roman occupation. The third was the famous Ninth, now based at York. The Fourteenth was effectively replaced by the Second Adiutrix after a short gap. The latter's departure reduced the garrison to three legions. The Sixth was brought over by Hadrian to assist in the construction of the famous wall in 122. Details concerning the fate of the Ninth are outside the scope of this book, although it will be briefly touched on in the next section. It was to play a major part in Cerialis' advance north.

Table 6: Roman legions in Britain

From AD 43	End of Nero's reign	Vespasian's reign	Post-Flavian period	Early 2nd to 4th century
Legio II Augusta	Legio II Augusta	Legio II Augusta	Legio II Augusta	Legio II Augusta
Legio XX Vatera Victrix	Legio XX Vatera Victrix	Legio XX Valeria Victrix	Legio XX Vatera Victrix	Legio XX Vatera Victrix
Legio IX Hispania	Legio IX Hispania	Legio IX Hispania	Legio IX Hispania (fate unknown)	
Legio XIV Gemina (left c. 64)				
		Legio II Adiutrix (left c. 87)		
				Legio VI Victrix (from c. 122)

It is known that Cerialis advanced as far north as Carlisle, Luguvalium, as tree-ring analysis dates felled trees to the year 72-3. Cerialis was succeeded by Frontius who pushed into the territory of the Silures in South Wales, who had held out for many years. A civitas capital was placed at Venta, Caerwent. This was a little to the east of a new legionary base at Isca, Caerleon. By 75 Vespasian had moved his old legion, *Legio II Augusta*, there. It became its permanent base throughout the next three centuries. The Twentieth, *Legio XX Valeria Victrix*, was posted to Wroxeter.

In late summer 77 Agricola was appointed provincial governor. The Ordivices in northern Wales were his first target and he subdued Anglesey. The following year he headed north into the territory of the Brigantes. By 79 he was extending even farther north from his base at Corbridge. When Titus came to power he ordered a halt at the Clyde-Forth isthmus but, by 81, he began a campaign into new territory against previously unknown tribes. This was to culminate in the battle of Mons Graupius under Domitian in c. 83, a devastating defeat for the northern Britons but Agricola was eventually to retreat to the Tyne-Solway isthmus. There a line of forts and a road, The Stanegate, were constructed. This became a relatively stable frontier for several decades and marked the line Hadrian took to build his famous wall.

Table 7: Flavian governors of Britain

Year	Governor	Appointed by
69-71	Marcus Vettius Bolanus	Nero
71-73/74	Quintus Pettilius Cerialis	Vespasian
73/74-77	Sextus Julius Frontius	Vespasian
77-84	Gnaeus Julius Agricola	Vespasian
84-93	Lucius Sallustius Lucullus	Domitian
c. 93	Aulus Vicirius Proculus	Domitian
c. 96	Publius Metilius Nepos	Domitian

Cassius Dio tells us that Agricola was the first to discover the fact that Britain was an island. Some mutinous soldiers had rebelled and, after killing the centurions and a military tribune, stole some boats and found themselves almost back where they started. Agricola sent others to attempt the voyage and confirmed it.

Under Vespasian, Agricola pushed the frontier to the Clyde-Forth isthmus, roughly along the route of the later Antonine Wall. The reign of Titus was short, just two years and Agricola's victory at Mons Graupius came under Domitian. Tacitus is critical of Domitian's subsequent policy: 'Britain was completely conquered and immediately let go.' The Romans withdraw to the Solway-Tyne isthmus, maintaining a few forward forts north of what became the Stanegate Road.

Table 8 shows the major campaigns under Vespasian and his sons. Figure 60 maps the major changes over this period.

Table 8: Flavian campaigns in Britain

Year	Governor	
71-3	Cerialis	Annexed Brigantian territory as far north as Carlisle. Tacitus describes 'many battles, some not unbloody'. Ninth Legion moved to York.
73-7	Frontius	Defeated Silures in South Wales. Pushed into Ordovices territory in northern Wales. Legionary forts built at Caerleon and Chester.
77-8	Agricola	Defeated Ordovices, slaying 'almost the whole nation'. Invaded Anglesey, deserting Druidic heartland.
79	Agricola	Pushed north 'as far as the Tay'.
80	Agricola	Consolidated Forth-Clyde isthmus.
81	Agricola	Pushed into Dumfries and Galloway in south-west Scotland 'as far as the sea' and surveyed Ireland from the coast.
82	Agricola	Advanced into Caledonia with three columns. Ninth Legion nearly destroyed in night attack.
83	Agricola	Battle of Mons Graupius
84	Agricola	Agricola recalled and Domitian 'let go' the hard-won gains.

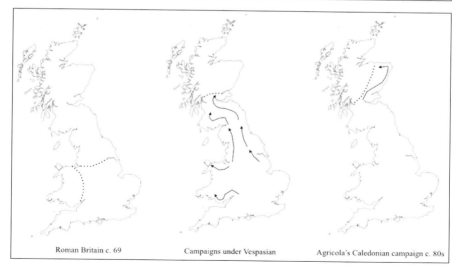

Roman Britain c. 69   Campaigns under Vespasian   Agricola's Caledonian campaign c. 80s

Figure 60: Roman Britain under the Flavians.

In summary it could be argued that Britain was far from secure when Vespasian came to power. Less than two decades had passed since Boudicca's revolt very nearly pushed the Romans out of Britain completely. Nero apparently considered abandoning the province altogether. It was under Vespasian that the Romans finally pushed west into Wales as far as the Irish Sea. But it was perhaps in the north that the greatest changes were felt. The powerful Brigantes came under Roman control early in Vespasian's reign. South of a line along what became the Stanegate Road remained under Roman rule for more than the next three centuries. It was along this very line that Hadrian was to build his wall half a century later.

Under Vespasian Agricola pushed as far north as the Tay. It took another sixty years, during the reign of Antoninus Pius, for the northern border to return to the Clyde-Forth isthmus. But for Domitian's decision to withdraw south, Agricola's victory at Mons Graupius might have heralded a new addition to the province, Roman Caledonia. Agricola even felt confident enough to claim that he could have invaded Ireland with a single legion and some auxiliaries.

It is interesting to wonder how history might have turned if the Romans had indeed conquered both main islands and remained for 300 years. Equally, a different Emperor from Vespasian may have gone one step further than Nero and left Britain to its own devices. Vespasian extended and secured Roman rule for the next three centuries.

The Ninth Legion

The fate of the Ninth Legion has fascinated scholars for many years. It was the basis of a famous book, *The Eagle of the Ninth*, by Rosemary Sutcliffe which in turn inspired the 2011 film, *The Eagle*. Whilst Rosemary Sutcliffe's book presents a possible scenario, the evidence, such as it exists, doesn't fully support the theory. Simon Elliott in *Roman Britain's Missing Legion, What Really Happened to IX Hispana?* summarises the evidence as follows:[8]

- The last reference to the legion is by Tacitus who has it campaigning with Agricola in the north of Britain in c. 82. (Agricola 25-7)
- The legion was apparently present at the battle of Mons Graupius in c. 83-4

- The last inscription in Britain is dated to 108 at York. (RIB 665)
- A vexillation of the Ninth was posted to the legionary fortress at Nijmergen in the province of *Germania Inferior* dated 104-120.
- The Sixth Legion arrived in Britain in 122.
- Inscriptions detailing units of the Second, Twentieth and Sixth legions show they took an active part in the construction of Hadrian's Wall c. 122-8. However, no such inscriptions exist for the Ninth, suggesting it did not take part or was not there.
- The legion is missing from the *Collonetta Maffei* list of legions in 168 (CIL VI.3492)

This places its disappearance sometime between 108-168. Elliott goes on to list various options which include:[9]

- Destroyed during a serious military crisis in the north of Britain between Hadrian's accession and his arrival in Britain, 117-122.
- A 'Hadrianic War' in London based on archaeological evidence of hundreds of skulls dated to c. 120-160s but proposed to be during early years of Hadrian's reign.
- The legion was lost fighting on the Rhine near where the vexillation was stationed.
- Alternatively, it was destroyed elsewhere, possibly in the east. For example, Trajan's Parthian War of 115; the Third Bar Kokhba Jewish Revolt, 132-5; or the Parthian War of 161-6.

Three main options include: destroyed by military defeat, disbandment or *damnatio memoriae*. Elliott suggests the end may have come in the north of Britain in the early years of Hadrian's reign. A combination of defeat and disbandment may have been the catalyst which prompted Hadrian's visit and the transfer of the Sixth.

However, epigraphical evidence suggest it may have survived into the second quarter of the second century. Birley lists the careers of a number of its officers after its apparent disappearance from the record in 108.[10] He notes references to *vexillatio Britannica* in Germania Inferior but also evidence from tile stamps at Carlisle. It is thus possible that it was sent farther north after the arrival at York of the Sixth. He suggests it may have remained in Britain for a further ten years or more and, possibly, was sent to the Jewish War of c. 134-6, or Cappodocia c. 137.

Following from this latter date an unnamed legion was destroyed at Elegia in the beginning of the Parthian War of 161-6, led by the governor of Cappodocia.

A number of legions are known to have been destroyed or disbanded, yet the Ninth is the only one whose fate is unknown.[11] Thus the mystery remains. We appear to be left with two leading contenders: It was lost in the north of Britain in the early years of Hadrian's reign, 117-122, or it remained in Britain for a few years before being transferred to Germany and was lost or disbanded some time before 168. Whatever the case, this left Britain with three legions, the Sixth based at York, the Second Augusta at Caerleon, and the Twentieth at Chester.

Vespasian's vice

After a turbulent year and a half of civil war and emperors dying like flies the empire appeared grateful for a period of calm. Militarily, Vespasian had proved himself as successful an emperor as he had been as a general. Not only were Judea and the Rhine pacified, but Roman legions were pressing forward in Britain. The mob, and society in general, were always happy with news of military success, even more so when it involved newly conquered land.

In the first century BC senators such as Cato were enraged by Caesar's illegal, as they saw it, wars in Gaul. But they were greatly outnumbered by those who eagerly read every snippet of news and Caesar's own reports. Vespasian no doubt was himself, as a young boy, thrilled at reports of the campaigns of Germanicus in Germania.

News of the defeat of a legion and loss of an eagle in Judea would have horrified Romans under Nero. But perhaps the Batavian revolt would have caused greater anguish. This was a bit too close for comfort. The ghosts of Varus's defeat in the Teutoburg Forest still haunted the minds of Romans, as did the historical fear of barbarians crossing the Rhine and threatening Italy itself. Now the mob could read of victories in far off Britannia. This was much better news for a new emperor than rampaging Germans raiding deep into nearby provinces in Gaul.

Additionally, sophisticated Romans such as Terence might scoff at the mob's obsession with gladiatorial contests, but emperors knew what garnered the most support. Just as modern politicians can smell which issues might provide a rich seam of votes, triumphs and gladiatorial shows brought the circuses. The loyalty of the eastern legions, and Egypt in particular, brought the bread. The building of the Amphitheatre brought hope for the future. It was a physical representation of Rome's continued greatness growing brick by brick.

Another important pillar for any regime is money. As many a would be candidate might say today, 'it's the economy, stupid.' Vespasian inherited a difficult financial situation but it was one he recognised and went about ruthlessly trying to deal with it. He reinstated taxes abolished by Galba and added new swingeing ones. Tribute from the provinces was significantly increased, in some cases doubled.

One criticism Suetonius levels at Vespasian is a 'love of money'. He was said to use men as sponge: 'soaked them when they were dry and squeezed them when they were wet.' This was a reference to promoting certain procurators who paid through the nose, only to confiscate their goods later when they were condemned and removed from office. When his son, Titus, criticised his tax on public lavatories, he held a coin under his son's nose, and asked if its odour was offensive to him. When Titus said 'No,' he replied, 'Yet it comes from urine'. Cassius Dio's account has him asking, 'See, my son, if they have any smell?' When people voted to erect a statue costing a million sesterces he held out his hand and said 'Give me the money; this is its pedestal.' More shocking still was an emperor buying commodities only to sell them later at a profit. Offices and acquittals were sold regardless of whether they deserved either.

Yet Suetonius grudgingly accepted that the state was in much need of serious finances (40,000,000,000 sesterces according to Vespasian) and the emperor made good use of the money he collected. Cities damaged by earthquakes were rebuilt and the arts and other talents were promoted. Vespasian was the first to establish a regular salary of 100,000 sesterces for Latin and Greek teachers of rhetoric, paid from the privy purse. In summary, Vespasian was every bit as successful in stabilising the economic situation as he was with the empire's borders.

One man's vice is another's virtue. Vespasian had already proved he had a level of integrity when he served as governor. Here we must put against the criticism of Suetonius the economic situation and outcome of Vespasian's polices. Vespasian inherited an extremely difficult financial situation that was potentially destabilising. That he managed to turn the ship of state around is testament to his policies. We can forgive his prudent careful approach given that he left the state's finances in better health than he found it.

Anti-semitism

There is perhaps a more serious stain on Vespasian's character than a level of miserliness. It has been suggested Vespasian developed a 'virulent hatred of Jews'.[12] Scholars point to Vespasian as a turning point for the evolution of Christianity and the birth of a virulent form of anti-semitism that was to haunt Europe across the centuries.[13]

Whilst the Roman gods of the established state religion remained dominant there was a renaissance of Egyptian gods outside Egypt. Additionally Christianity changed from being an obscure sect of Judaism to something rather distinct. It took the Roman-Jewish War and destruction of the temple to create the context where early Christians no longer looked to Jerusalem as the centre of their church. It laid the groundwork for a religion now independent of Judaism and one with often 'pernicious hostility to them'.

For Judaism the Diaspora was reinforced but it was perhaps the destruction of the temple that had the most significant effect. Cassius Dio records that from that time 'the Jews who continued to observe their ancestral customs should pay an annual tribute of two denarii to Jupiter Capitolinus'. A worse fate befell many of the captives. Titus celebrated his brother's birthday in Cesarea by inflicting, 'a great deal of the punishment for the Jews'. Over 2,500 were thrown to the beasts in the arena, forced to fight one another in gladiatorial bouts or burnt alive for the entertainment of the crowd. Perhaps as many as ten thousand were killed overall and still the mob considered the punishment 'beneath their deserts'. The sources tell us much of the cost of Vespasian's building works, the Colosseum in particular, came from the Jewish War.

Against this charge other defeated people received equally harsh treatment. Roman history is littered with massacres, destroyed towns and enslaved populations. It is unlikely any other people, culture or religion, having stood up to Rome and against its gods, would have received a different fate.

Personal life

Vespasian's wife, Flavia Domitilla, is thought to have died before he was acclaimed emperor in 69. She had been the mistress of an equestrian, Statilius Capella, from Sabrata in Africa. Suetonius described her low-birth: 'a woman originally only of Latin rank, but afterwards declared a free-born citizen of Rome'. Her father was a mere quaestor's clerk. They had three children, Titus, Domitian, and a daughter Flavia Domitilla, who also died before c. 69. It has been noted Domitilla may have been married to Cerialis, the general responsible for quelling the Batavia revolt and extending Roman rule in Britain.

Figure 61: Funerary altar of Antonia Caenis. (Wikimedia Commons)

Suetonius tells us that after the death of his wife he resumed his relations with Caenis, the freedwoman of Antonia, Emperor Caligula's grandmother. Caenis had formerly been his mistress and we are told even after he became emperor he treated her 'almost as a lawful wife'.

Caenis died in 74 and Cassius Dio provides further detail, describing her as 'a remarkable woman'. She was 'exceedingly faithful' and had an excellent memory. Vespasian took 'excessive delight in her' and allowed her significant influence. She was able to amass untold wealth selling governorships, procuratorships, generalships and priesthoods. Some suspected that whilst Caenis received the money it ended up with Vespasian. Whatever the case Vespasian appears to have trusted her implicitly.

Personality and appearance

Vespasian was described as 'well built, with strong sturdy limbs'. He had a serious, almost strained expression that one wit remarked made him looked as though he was on the toilet. He had good health and had spent

Figure 62: Gold aureus of Vespasian c. AD 70. (Wikimedia Commons)

many years of his life on campaign, in Britain and later in Judea. He was a hard working emperor, rising early and retiring to bed late.

He always rose very early, in fact before daylight. His first act was to read his correspondence before seeing friends, such as the famous writer Pliny the Elder. After completing his morning's work he would relax with one of the many women he kept after the death of his long-time lover Caenis. After dealing with business he rode before taking a nap. After this siesta he bathed and then went to the dining-room. Here he was most good-natured and indulgent and petitioners had the best chance of having requests granted. An affable and witty man he comes across as someone who did not take himself too seriously.

Given his reported love of money it is perhaps apt to use a gold aureus to provide a final image of Vespasian.

Vespasian's death

The end came in his favourite spot in Cutiliae near Raete, close to his childhood home, where he spent every summer. Already ill he contracted a bowel complaint. When he was very sick and he suspected near-death he quipped: 'Woe is me I think I am becoming a god'. He continued to perform his duties and received embassies even when bed-ridden. He was struck with a sudden bout of diarrhoea which almost rendered him unconscious. Cassius Dio over a century later tells us he died 'not of his accustomed gout' but of a fever.

Vespasian struggled to get up, declaring: 'An emperor ought to die standing.' As he did so he collapsed, dying in the arms of those helping him. He was 69 years old and eight months and had reigned for six days short of ten years. Later accusations of foul play were dismissed by Dio as designed by enemies to falsely accuse Titus.

Suetonius stated that the Flavian dynasty gave the empire new strength after the Year of the Four Emperors had left it in a precarious state. Nero, Galba, and Vitellius had all been slaughtered within a year with Otho taking his own life. Tacitus viewed him as a realist who had a sense of proportion and humour.[14] Ironically he had no time for gladiatorial shows or 'civilian fantasies' having experienced the reality of battle many times.

Levick lists the main achievements:[15] Restoration of peace; building programme in Rome; and the reconquest of Judea. He strove for 'order and hierarchy, a sense of moral values and the idea of continuity'. The destruction of Jerusalem may have been viewed as an achievement by the Romans and Medieval Christians looked favourably on a man who was a 'scourge of the Jews' and viewed the Colosseum as 'unstained by Christian blood'.[16] Leonardo de Vinci described him as a 'life put to good use' and Napoleon viewed him as one of the greatest men Rome ever produced.

His merits included a disinclination to allow resentment to cloud his judgement. He did not make rash decisions but when he made his mind up he tended to follow it through. A stable man who was not easily panicked into impulsive actions. He understood his power lay in the army and humiliating his opponents gained nothing and potentially

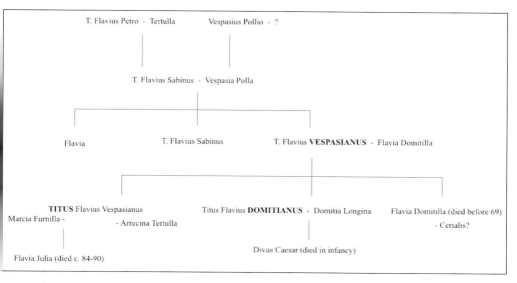

Figure 63: The Flavian Dynasty.

created more problems through resentment. He founded a dynasty which, though relatively short-lived, formed the foundation of stable government for another century.

Table 9: Key dates in Vespasian's life

Year	
9	Birth of Vespasian
14	Death of Augustus, Tiberius Emperor
c. 25-6	Vespasian receives *toga virilis*
c. 27	Vespasian military tribune in Thrace
c. 32	Vespasian obtains first magistracy: Triumvir Capitalis
c. 35-6	Vespasian appointed Quaestor in Crete and Cyrenaica.
37	Tiberius dies, Caligula Emperor
38	Vespasian appointed Aedile
39	Titus born
c. 40	Vespasian appointed praetor
41	Caligula assassinated, Claudius emperor
42	Vespasian appointed commander of II Augusta
43	Vespasian takes part in invasion of Britain
43-7	Vespasian subdues south western Britain. Receives triumphal ornaments
49	Claudius marries Agrippina and adopts Nero
51	Vespasian suffect consul, Domitian born.
54	Death of Claudius, Nero emperor
59	Agrippina killed
62-3	Vespasian appointed pro-consul of Africa
c. 65-66	Vespasian leaves Nero's court in Greece
66	Revolt in Judea, Vespasian appointed *legatus Augusti pro praetore exercitus Iudaici*, Propraetorian Legate of the Army of Judea
67	Vespasian arrives in Judea, siege of Jotapata

Year	
68	Vespasian continues campaign across Judea. Revolt of Vindex. Nero dies, Galba emperor.
69	Vitellius declared emperor by Rhine legions. Batavian revolt. Galba killed, Otho declared emperor in Rome. Battle of Bedriacum, Otho dies. 1st July Vespasian declared emperor in east. Flavian army victors at 2nd battle of Bedriacum. Vitellius killed in Rome. Vespasian declared emperor.
70	Vespasian returns to Rome End of Batavian revolt Jerusalem captured by Titus
71	Triumph of Vespasian and Titus
73	Last stronghold of Masada in Judea taken
77	Agricola appointed governor of Britain
79	Vespasian dies. Titus emperor. Eruption of Vesuvius.
81	Titus dies, Domitian emperor (dies 96)

Chapter 8

LEGACY

Vespasian was succeeded by Titus, his eldest son. Many feared he would prove to be a second Nero. They would be pleasantly surprised. Suetonius would later describe him as the 'delight and darling of the human race'.[1] This despite attracting much public criticism and even hatred during his father's reign.

He was born in 39 and was three years old when his father led the Second Augusta across southern Britain. Despite a slight 'protruding belly' and a lack of height he was described as a 'handsome person'. Court flattery perhaps, the Flavians were not noted for their beauty. His father had been the soldiers' soldier and it appears with Titus the apple didn't fall far from the tree. Unusually strong and physically accomplished he was a skilled horseman and adept at arms. Additionally his memory is reported to have been extraordinary. Another quirky talent was the ability to write shorthand with great speed and imitate another's handwriting calling himself 'the prince of forgers'. He also wrote verses and speeches in Latin and Greek.

As a boy he had been close to Britannicus, the son of Claudius and his doomed third wife, Valeria Messalina.

It was claimed Titus was sitting next to him when he was allegedly poisoned by Agrippina. So close in fact that he had supped from the same wine and very nearly succumbed himself. He barely survived and was reported to have been ill for some time after. Britannicus died the day before his fourteenth birthday and his best friend would have been fifteen years old. He never forgot his friend and years later set up a golden statue and dedicated another equestrian statue of ivory in his honour.

Like his father his career was dented by Agrippina's hostility to anyone not perceived loyal. However he was still very young when the emperor's mother died and by his early twenties he had served as a military tribune both in Germany and in Britain. The position of *tribunus laticlavius* was the first step on the *cursus honorum* for a young man of senatorial rank. There he won 'a high reputation for energy and no less integrity'. Given no mention of the Boudiccan revolt in c. 60-1 it is likely he arrived after events, perhaps in c. 62-3, and had taken part in the re-pacification of the province.

Whatever the case he was soon back in Rome as he became quaestor in c. 65. The outbreak of the Judean War gave Titus the opportunity to shine, albeit alongside his experienced father. Commanding a legion he captured the cities of Tarichaeae and Gamala. He lived up to the reputation of his father, even having a horse killed under him in the midst of battle.

When Jerusalem fell in his father's first year as emperor the troops hailed Titus as *imperator*. Wagging tongues claimed he had aspirations on his father's throne. This was further fuelled when he wore a diadem en route to Alexandria. His explanation was this was in accordance with the local customer rituals of the ancient cult of the bull Apis at Memphis. Titus was as politically astute as his father and realised appearance was as importance as truth and rushed back to Rome. Once there he celebrated a joint triumph and consulship with Vespasian. He seems to have squashed any rumours as Suetonius described him as from that moment on acting as the emperor's partner and guardian.

His reign when it started began with two ill-omened events. Firstly Mount Vesuvius erupted on 24 August 79 destroying the towns of Pompeii and Herculaneum. The dust was said to to have reached as far as Africa and Syria and even Egypt. Rome, being much closer, experienced greater effects. The air was filled with dust, darkening the very sun for several days. This was followed by a terrible pestilence. The following year a huge fire spread through the capital. The list of buildings destroyed read like a tourist guide to first century Rome: The Baths of Agrippa; Pompey's Theatre; the Pantheon; the Diribitorium; and Octavian buildings containing priceless books.

The very gods themselves seemed displeased. The temples of Serapis, Isis, Saepta and Neptune all were consumed. Worse was the loss of the Temple of Jupiter. The very same temple that had been destroyed during the Flavian attack which had ended Vitellius's reign. Rebuilt by Vespasian a superstitious mind might wonder if the Flavians were truly blessed by the gods. This did not prevent Titus deifying his father six months after his death.

Despite this inauspicious start Titus was to receive a good press from contemporary historians. Perhaps one reason for his popularity was the games he put on for the mob. The most extravagant being the inaugural games in his father's main building project.

The Flavian Hunting Theatre

The Hunting Theatre, as it was known then, had taken nearly a decade to build. Laying at the foot of the Palatine Hill, a short walk from the Forum. Just north of the imposing structure Titus had constructed an impressive Bath House, *Thermae Titi*. Between the two structures rose a huge bronze statue, 100 feet high intended to represent Nero (known as *Colossus Neronis*). Vespasian had spent a large sum on a new head, that of Helios the original of the Colossus of Rhodes. One theory is it is this statue that gave the Flavian Hunting Theatre its alternative title, Colosseum. Hadrian would later move this to the west of the Colosseum so that it would greet visitors walking from the Forum.

The inaugural games were to last 100 days. Cassius Dio describes the events:[2] nine thousand animals, 'both tame and wild', were killed, equating to 90 a day. A strange sounding battle between cranes and four elephants were among the entertainments. Notably, women took part in the beast hunts at least.

Gladiators fought both in single combat and in groups. Here we get an indication the arena was able to be flooded: 'For Titus suddenly filled this same theatre with water'. Horses and bulls and 'other domesticated animals' had been trained to move in water although what the exact entertainment was is not explained. Perhaps more thrilling was the naval battles. One example involved a reenactment of a battle between the Corcyreans and Corinthians.

Suetonius places a sea battle in the 'Old Naumachia'. This has caused some historians to doubt Cassius Dio on this point. Keith Hopkins and Mary Beard, in *The Colosseum*, claims that such an event was not possible in the building as it survives today.[3] The basements could not be waterproofed for one thing. Yet Dio also makes a point that a similar nautical display also took place outside the city in 'the grove of Gaius and Lucius'. The first emperor, Augustus, had excavated a large area for this very purpose.

This lake was able to be be covered over by a platform of wooden planks surrounded by wooden stands for spectators. The platform was not only strong enough for gladiators and beast hunts but on the second day a horse race took place. The next day the platform was removed and a naval battle involving 3,000 men took place followed by an infantry battle. This reenacted the conflict between Athens and Syracuse 415-413 BC during the Peloponnesian War. The Athenians landed on an island in the middle and attacked a wall defended by those taking the part of the Syracusians.

A second reenactment, this time of the great sea-battle between Corcyra and Corinth, took place. The Battle of Sybota, 433 BC was an epic showdown as 150 Corinthian ships faced off against 110 ships of their former colony who were aided by a small force of 10 Athenian vessels. The battle was indecisive and was part of the beginnings of the Peloponnesian War.

To add further entertainment Titus had small wooden balls dropped from above in to the crowd. Each was inscribed with a prize of some sort: some article of food, clothing, a silver vessel or perhaps a gold one, even horses, pack-animals, cattle or slaves. These could be exchanged after the show for the prizes written upon them.

The poet Martial described some typical events. It is here we read of the re-enactment of the legend of the Minotaur. We recall King Minos of Crete was punished by the god Poseidon when he forced the king's wife, Pasiphae, to couple with a bull. The resultant off-spring was the legendary monster of the labyrinth. Quite how the Romans conducted this is not made clear. There are certainly accounts of beasts being trained to perform various unsavoury tasks. But perhaps it is more likely someone simply dressed as a bull acted out the scene. We can only hope the victim was also acting.

We can have less doubt over the unfortunate Laureolus. the sorts of crimes that led to his dreadful fate were helpfully listed for similar criminals: thrusting a sword through his father's or master's throat, stealing a temple's gold or arson. Perhaps Laureolus had committed all three as he was a 'thug', a 'wicked man', who had outstripped the crimes of ancient times'. Martial is in no doubt he deserved his punishment. Hung from a cross (possibly crucified) a ferocious Caledonian bear was set upon his 'uncovered entrails'. He seems to have been disembowelled to encourage the bear. Torn limb for limb, bloody stumps dripping blood, the bear ate him alive.

Figure 64: Colossal head of Titus c. 79–81. (Wikimedia Commons)

Lions were a common entertainment. One turned on its handler and was dispatched with javelins. A second was trained to allow a hand placed in his mouth. Something inside him snapped and he reverted to his natural state, turning on two young boys who were raking the arena's blood-soaked sand. Martial seems horrified by this and we can only guess the boys were killed. An unscripted act on two innocents was not the entertainment the crowd appreciated. Another lion, possibly re-enacting a deed of Hercules, was killed by 'a woman's hand', a novelty for the crowd.

A bear was pierced through, receiving a wound by a 'weighty javelin'. Perhaps this was the same bear that was trained to hold a boy's hand in its gaping jaws but ripped it off when a viper distracted it. Elephants, a favourite of the crowd, were trained to kneel before the emperor. Water beasts, 'formerly unknown', were displayed and we read that Triton's chariot 'seethed in the water' while a certain Nereus found himself 'walking on foot amid the limpid waters'.

The inaugural games were a roaring success. The Flavian Hunting Theatre enabled successive emperors to provide the mob with one half of the 'bread and circuses' referenced by Decimus Junius Juvenalis in *Satires*, c. 100. A century later Commodus would famously, and scandalously, take to the sand himself. The Colosseum perhaps best symbolises Vespasian's legacy. He did not live to see the opening ceremony. But he laid the foundation of a stable empire that was to survive for centuries to come.

Death of Titus

The new emperor did not survive long after the inaugural games of Colosseum. He left for his Sabine estate where he was stricken with a fever. Titus gets a good press from Suetonius: he respected property, took 'nothing from any citizen' and wouldn't even accept gifts. Yet he was extremely generous. He had some bad luck, having to deal with three serious emergencies in his reign: the eruption of Mount Vesuvius; a fire in Rome which lasted three days and nights; and a plague 'the like of which had hardly ever been known before'.

When he died at the age of 41 Suetonius declared it 'the loss of mankind'. Just before he died he is reported to have said he had only one regret. Unfortunately he did not state what it was and so we are left to speculate. One suggestion at the time was he had slept with Domitia, his brother's wife. Both Suetonius and Cassius Dio reject this with the latter suggesting that it was the fact 'he had not killed Domitian when he found him openly plotting against him'.[4] Dio goes on to say 'the whole populace mourned as they would for a loss in their own families'.

Domitian

No sooner had Titus died rumours of foul play emerged. Suspicion fell on his younger brother Domitian. The sources reference continuous plots. Titus's last words, that he regretted only one thing, were never explained. This allowed gossips and conspiracy theorists to speculate. Had Titus taken his brother's wife, Domitia, as a lover? She swore a denial. Still, according to Suetonius during his brother's reign Domitian complained he had been cheated out of a part-share of the empire by a forged will.

Domitian was to rule longer than his father and brother combined. Yet his rule ended in ignominy and murder. An able administrator he attempted to raise standards of government, downgrading jurors who accepted bribes. He turned his ire on public morality punishing senators who practised homosexuality and baiting the castration of males. Vestal Virgins were condemned to death for proving unable to live up to their title. The Chief Vestal, Cornelia, suffered the traditional penalty of being buried alive.

Domitian's autocratic style can be seen in his adopting the title, *dominus et deus*, 'lord and god'. The great victory of Agricola over the Caledonians at Mons Graupius was followed by other successful wars. Victory over the Chatti earned Domitian the title *Germanicus*. Reversals against the Dacians resulted in the death of a governor and a legionary legate in two separate engagements. By 89 the Dacians had been forced to come to

Figure 65: Bust of Domitian. (Wikimedia Commons)

terms and the Romans turned their attentions to the Quadi, Marcomanni and Sarmatians, all tribes north of the Danube.

Unrest at his reign can be seen in attempted plots in 87 and 89. By 93 Domitian was insecure and paranoid enough to visit a reign of terror on senators, equestrians and officials. Death and exile were common place.

His end came in the year 96 by which time his cruelty had made him 'an object of terror and hatred'. Trusted freedmen, friends and even his own wife conspired against him. He was stabbed to death in his bedchamber by his attendants and steward.

Conclusion

When Vespasian was born the first emperor Augustus had already stamped his authority on the empire. Republican sentiment may well have lingered but imperial rule seemed unassailable. His immediate successor, Tiberius, was stable enough but the reigns of Caligula and Nero strained the sinews that facilitated stable government. As much as Augustus had been competent and astute, Caligula and Nero had been negligent and self absorbed. In many ways Vespasian was a return to Augustus. Elderly Romans old enough to remember would have appreciated the new emperor's mature no-nonsense approach to government.

True, the ascension of Galba had broke a taboo. If one general could be declared emperor by his troops why not another? If the senate could be bent to the will of the army or praetorians on one occasion then there was nothing to stop a repeat. Future emperors would indeed be made and broken in this way. But why break something that wasn't broken?

Vespasian's rule worked and was seen and felt to work where it mattered most. The army, the senate and the mob. Where previous emperors had lost support in one or all sections of society Vespasian was careful and astute enough to keep enough people content.

It is worth comparing Vespasian's legacy with another usurping general. Over a century after Vespasian's death another legate rose to power from the ashes of civil war, Septimius Severus, 193-211. The last of the Five Good Emperors, Marcus Aurelius had died in 180. Commodus, like Domitian was to die from a plot by his closest advisors in 193. Not in the Colosseum at the hands of Maximus Decimius Meridius as in Gladiator, 'husband to a murdered wife…'. Rather in the bath at the hands of his wrestling partner after a failed poisoning. Pertinax lasted three months before the praetorians butchered him in his palace. The year 193 saw another year of multiple emperors. This time the 'year of the Five Emperors'.

Didius Julianus in Rome succeeding Commodus, Clodius Albinus in Britain, Pescennius Niger in Syria and Septimius Severus on the Danube. Ultimately Severus was the one to prevail. Like Vespasian he also was succeeded by two sons, Caracalla and Geta. As it turns out Caracalla was more murderous than Domitian proved to be and killed his own brother within the year. Like Domitian Caracalla too was killed. Stabbed in the back, quite literally, while relieving himself on the roadside.

However there the comparisons end. The following hundred years after Caracalla's murder was marked by a succession of failed rulers, major defeats and what became known as the Crisis of the Third Century. Civil war and murdered emperors litter the decades and the empire broke into pieces on more than one occasion.

This could easily have been the fate of Rome in the first century. Yet the Flavian dynasty, even with Domitian's legacy, was succeeded not by a repeat of the year 69 but by decades of stable government. Vespasian was undoubtedly the best emperor since Augustus. More amiable than Tiberius, more professional and conscientious than either Caligula and Nero. Without Vespasian Rome may not have had a succession of well liked and efficient emperors.

He inherited an empire racked with civil war, economic difficulties, chaotic unstable government and two major internal revolts.

He provided stable government and a sound economy. The empire was to last many centuries but perhaps its greatest period was the century after Vespasian's death. A period which ended with the demise of Marcus Aurelius. An event described by Cassius Dio as symbolising the change from a 'Kingdom of Gold to one of iron and rust'. One could argue that Vespasian inherited a 'Kingdom of iron and rust' and would lay the foundation for the very 'Kingdom of Gold' Cassius Dio admired so much.

IMAGE SOURCES

Figure 1: Uniform of a first century legate (Steven Cockings)

Figure 2: Bust of Vespasian (Wikimedia Commons)
CC BY-SA 4.0, https://commons.wikimedia.org/w/index.php?curid=85595151

Figure 3: Altar panel c. 2nd century depicting Romulus and Remus (Wikimedia Commons)
Representation of the *lupercal*: Romulus and Remus fed by the she-wolf, Lupa, surrounded by representations of the Tiber and the Palatine. Panel from an altar dedicated to the divine couple of Mars and Venus. Marble, Roman artwork of the end of the reign of Trajan (98-117 CE), later re-used under the Hadrianic era (117-132 CE) as a base for a statue of Silvan. From the portico of the Piazzale dei Corporazioni in Ostia Antica. Shown in museum of Palazzo Massimo alle Terme (Rome). By Marie-Lan Nguyen (2006), Public Domain, https://commons.wikimedia.org/w/index.php?curid=1233398

Figure 10 The Roman Empire at the time of Augustus Caesar. (Wikimedia Commons). CC BY-SA 3.0, https://commons.wikimedia.org/w/index.php?curid=2452303

Figure 11: The Rhine Frontier (Wikimedia Commons)
CC BY-SA 3.0, https://commons.wikimedia.org/w/index.php?curid=3987397

Figure 14: Model of Roman Trireme, Wikimedia Commons, CC BY-SA 2.0 fr, https://commons.wikimedia.org/w/index.php?curid=64322

Figure 15: Map of Roman Empire under Caligula (Wikimedia Commons). By Homoatrox - Own work, based on File:Blank map of South Europe and North Africa.svg (CC-BY-SA-3.0), CC BY-SA 4.0, https://commons.wikimedia.org/w/index.php?curid=62667183

Figure17: Re-enactment of 1st century Briton (Owain Edwards) outside roundhouse at Castell Henllys Iron-Age Village, Wales. Author's photo with permission of Owain Edwards.

Figure 18: Reconstruction of typical 1st century roundhouses at Castell Henllys Iron-Age Village Wales. Author's photo with permission of Owain Edwards.

Figure 24: Aerial view of Maiden Castle (Wikimedia commons) https://commons.wikimedia.org/w/index.php?curid=12228040

Figure 25: Ramparts at Maiden Castle (Wikimedia commons). By Nilfanion - Wikimedia UK, CC BY-SA 4.0, https://commons.wikimedia.org/w/index.php?curid=47632244

Figure 26: Roman *testudo* formation from Trajan's Column (Wikimedia commons). By Cassius Ahenobarbus - Own work, CC BY-SA 3.0, https://commons.wikimedia.org/w/index.php?curid=104683968

Figure 27: Reproduction of Roman Ballista (Wikimedia commons). By Rolf Krahl - dsc_3735, CC BY-SA 2.0, https://commons.wikimedia.org/w/index.php?curid=42587336

Figure 28: Drawing of a Roman onager (Wikimedia commons). Author: Hermann Diels (1848-1922) - Antike Technik: Sechs Vorträge, Public Domain, https://commons.wikimedia.org/w/index.php?curid=37717934

Figure 29: Roman carroballista from column of Marcus Aurelius (Wikimedia commons). CC BY-SA 3.0, https://commons.wikimedia.org/w/index.php?curid=6077612

Figure 31: Legionary legate and legionaries of the Second Legion (Alisa Vanlint of Legio Secunda Augusta and Ludus Augusta)

Figure 32: Legionary wearing *lorica* hamata (Alisa Vanlint of Legio Secunda Augusta and Ludus Augusta)

Figure 33: A Briton dispatching a Roman soldier (Alisa Vanlint of Legio Secunda Augusta and Ludus Augusta)

Figure 34: Battle re-enactment. (Zane Green of Legio Secunda Augusta)

Figure 35: Battle re-enactment. (Zane Green of Legio Secunda Augusta)

Figure 36: Britons (Zane Green of Legio Secunda Augusta)

Figure 37: Britons (Zane Green of Legio Secunda Augusta)

Figure 38: Roman siege ramp at Masada. (Wikimedia Commons) CC BY-SA 3.0, https://commons.wikimedia.org/w/index.php?curid=3270974

Figure 39: Map of Vespasian's campaign in Judea (Wikimedia Commons). Adapted from: CC BY 3.0, https://commons.wikimedia.org/w/index.php?curid=9850463

Figure 40: Bust of Nero (Wikimedia Commons). https://commons.wikimedia.org/w/index.php?curid=1814923

Figure 41: Bust of Galba (Wikimedia Commons). CC BY 2.0, https://commons.wikimedia.org/w/index.php?curid=113466744

Figure 42: Bust of Otho (Wikimedia Commons). CC BY-SA 2.0, https://commons.wikimedia.org/w/index.php?curid=8834346

Figure 43: Bust of Vitellius (Wikimedia Commons). https://commons.wikimedia.org/w/index.php?curid=11933182

Figure 44: Bust of Vespasian (Wikimedia Commons). CC BY-SA 3.0, https://commons.wikimedia.org/w/index.php?curid=3244626

Figure 45: Map of the Roman Empire 68-9. (Wikimedia Commons) Modified version of Image:Baleares SPQR.png, CC BY-SA 3.0, https://commons.wikimedia.org/w/index.php?curid=3268261

Figure 47: Bust of Vespasian (Wikimedia commons). Heribert Pohl, CC BY-SA 2.0, https://commons.wikimedia.org/w/index.php?curid=34100478

Figure 48: Colosseum. (Wikimedia Commons) CC BY-SA 3.0, https://commons.wikimedia.org/w/index.php?curid=51319

Figure 49: Colosseum Interior. (Wikimedia Commons) CC BY-SA 3.0, https://commons.wikimedia.org/w/index.php?curid=132875

Figure 50: Hoplomachus vs Thraex. (Wikimedia Commons) Detail of the Gladiator mosaic floor, a Hoplomachus fighting a Thraex, Römerhalle, Bad Kreuznach, Germany. Author: Carole Raddato from FRANKFURT, Germany. Uploaded by Marcus Cyron, CC BY-SA 2.0, https://commons.wikimedia.org/w/index.php?curid=30157029

Figure 51: Thraex vs Murmillo. (Wikimedia Commons) Detail of Gladiator mosaic, a Thraex (left) fighting a Murmillo (right), Römerhalle, Bad Kreuznach, Germany. Author: Carole Raddato from FRANKFURT, Germany. Uploaded by Marcus Cyron, CC BY-SA 2.0, https://commons.wikimedia.org/w/index.php?curid=30157015

Figure 52: Provocator vs Provocator. (Wikimedia Commons) Author: Gladiatorenschule Berlin - Own work, CC BY-SA 4.0, https://commons.wikimedia.org/w/index.php?curid=87589097

Figure 53: Retiarius vs Secutor. (Wikimedia Commons) Mosaic showing a retiarius (net-fighter) named Kalendio fighting a secutor named Astyanax. The lanista, master of gladiators, cheers them on. The outcome is shown above and confirmed by the inscriptions; the word VICIT appears beside Astyanax, and beside Kalendio's name is an O with a line through it, an abbreviation for Obiit or death. 3rd century AD, National Archaeological Museum of Spain, Madrid. Author: Carole Raddato from FRANKFURT, Germany -, CC BY-SA 2.0, https://commons.wikimedia.org/w/index.php?curid=37878968

Figure 54: Scissor vs Retiarius. (Wikimedia Commons) Retiarius and Scissor in a show fight in Carnuntum 2015. Author: MatthiasKabel -

Own work, CC BY-SA 4.0, https://commons.wikimedia.org/w/index. php?curid=59809470

Figure 55: Eques vs Eques. (Wikimedia Commons) Detail of Gladiator mosaic, two Eques fighting equipped with lance, sword and the traditional small round shield, Römerhalle, Bad Kreuznach, Germany. Author: Carole Raddato from FRANKFURT, Germany. Uploaded by Marcus Cyron, CC BY-SA 2.0, https://commons.wikimedia.org/w/ index.php?curid=30157041

Figure 56: Mounted Eques. (Wikimedia Commons) Gladiator "eques" during a show in Carnuntum.
Author: MatthiasKabel - Own work, CC BY 2.5,https://commons. wikimedia.org/w/index.php?curid=2325276

Figure 57: Gladiators fighting. Photo from Alisa Vanlint of Legio Secunda Augusta and Ludus Augusta.

Figure 58: Gladiators fighting. Photo from Alisa Vanlint of Legio Secunda Augusta and Ludus Augusta.

Figure 61: Funerary altar of Antonia Caenis (Wikimedia Commons) CC BY-SA 3.0, https://commons.wikimedia.org/w/index. php?curid=6418862

Figure 62: Gold aureus of Vespasian c. AD 70 (Wikimedia Commons) CC0, https://commons.wikimedia.org/w/index.php?curid=60407717

Figure 64: Colossal head of Titus c. 79–81 (Wikimedia Commons) https://commons.wikimedia.org/w/index.php?curid=1888196

Figure 65: Bust of Domitian (Wikimedia Commons) https://commons.wikimedia.org/w/index.php?curid=1222636

REFERENCES

Aldrete, Gregory, and Sumner, Graham, *Ancient Rome on the Silver Screen*, (Rowman and Littlefield, Lanham, 2023).

Beard, Mary, *The Roman Triumph*, (Belknap Press, Cambridge, Massachusetts, 2009).

Beard, Mary, *SPQR A History of Ancient Rome*, (Profile Books, London, 2016). Berresford-Ellis, Peter, *Caesar's Invasion of Britain*, (Constable, London, 1994)

Birley, Anthony, *Garrison Life at Vindolanda, A Band of Brothers*, (Tempus, Stroud, 2002).

Birley, Anthony, *Septimius Severus the African Emperor*, (Routledge, London, 1999).

Birley, Anthony, *The Roman Government of Britain*, (Oxford University Press, Oxford, 2005).

Bishop, M.C., *Gladiators, Fighting to the Death in Ancient Rome,* (Casemate, Oxford, 2017).

Bishop, M.C., *The Secret History of the Roman Roads of Britain*, (Pen and Sword, Barnsley, 2020).

Bishop, M.C., *Lucius Verus and the Roman Defence of the East*, (Pen and Sword, Barnsley, 2018).

Breeze, David, J. and Dobson, Brian, *Hadrian's Wall*, (Penguin Books, London, 2000).

Breeze, David, *Edge of Empire, Rome's Scottish Frontier, The Antonine Wall*, (Birlinn, Edinburgh, 2008).

Breeze, David, *The Roman Army*, (Bloomsbury, London, 2016).

Bruun, Christer and Edmondson, Jonathan, *The Oxford Handbook of Roman Epigraphy*, (Oxford University Press, Oxford, 2015).

Caesar, *The Gallic War*, (Oxford University Press, Oxford, 2008).

Carver, Martin, *Formative Britain, An Archaeology of Britain, Fifth to Eleventh Century AD*, (Routledge, London, 2019).

References

Casey, P.J., *Carausius and Allectus*, (Yale University Press, New Haven, 1994).

Chrystal, Paul, *A Historical Guide to Roman York*, (Pen and Sword, Barnsley, 2021).

Collins, Rob, *Hadrian's Wall and the End of Empire*, (Routledge, New York, 2012).

Collins, Rob, *Living on the Edge of Empire*, (Pen and Sword, Barnsley, 2020).

Crook, J.A., *Law and Life of Rome, 90 BC – AD 212*, (Cornell University Press, New York, 1967).

Crow, James, *Housesteads Roman Fort*, (English Heritage, 2012).

Crummy, Philip, *City of Victory: The Story of Colchester - Britain's First Roman Town*, (Colchester Archaeological Trust, Colchester, 1997).

Cruse, Audrey, *Roman Medicine*, (Tempus, Stroud, 2004).

Cunliffe, Barry, *Britain Begins*, (Oxford University Press, Oxford, 2011).

Cunliffe, Barry, *The Ancient Celts*, (Oxford University Press, Oxford, 1997).

Czajkowski, Kimberley, Eckhardt, Benedikt, *Law in the Roman Provinces*, (Oxford University Press, Oxford, 2020).

Dando-Collins, Stephen, *Legions of Rome, The Definitive History of Every Imperial Roman Legion*, (Thomas Dunne Books, St Martin's Press, New York, 2010).

D'Amato, R. and Negin, A., *Decorated Roman Armour, from the Age of the Kings to the Death of Justinian the great*, (Frontline Books, Barnsley, 2017).

D'Amato, Raffaele and Sumner, Graham, *Arms and Armour of the Imperial Roman Soldier, from Marius to Commodus, 112 BC – AD 192*, (Frontline Books, London, 2009).

Davenport, Caillan, *A History of the Roman Equestrian Order*, (Cambridge University Press, Cambridge, 2019).

Davies, Hugh, *Roman Roads in Britain*, (Shire Archaeology, Oxford, 2008).

De La Bédoyère, Guy, *Eagles over Britannia*, (Tempus Publishing, Stroud, 2001).

De La Bédoyère, Guy, *Gladius, Living Fighting and Dying in the Roman Army*, (Little Brown, London, 2020).

De La Bédoyère, Guy, *Roman Britain, A New History*, (Thames and Hudson, London, 2006).

De La Bédoyère, Guy, *The Real Lives of Roman Britain*, (Yale University Press, New Haven, 2015).

Elliott, Paul, *Everyday Life of a Soldier on Hadrian's Wall*, (Fonthill, 2015).

Elliott, Simon, *Roman Conquests: Britain*, (Pen and Sword, Barnsley, 2021)

Elliott, Simon, *Roman Legionaries, Soldiers of Empire*, (Casemate, Oxford, 2018).

Elliott, Simon, *Romans at War*, (Casemate, Oxford, 2020).

Elliott, Simon, *Sea Eagles of Empire, The Classis Britannica and the Battles for Britain*, (History Press, Stroud, 2016).

Elliott, Simon, *Septimus Severus in Scotland*, (Greenhill Books, Barnsley, 2018).

Epplett, Christopher, *Gladiators and Beast Hunts, Arena Sports of Ancient Rome*, (Pen and Sword, Barnsley, 2016).

Esposito, Gabriele, *Armies of Celtic Europe 700 BC – AD 106*, (Pen and Sword, Barnsley, 2019).

Goldsworthy, Adrian, *Caesar*, (Phoenix, London, 2007)

Goldsworthy, Adrian, *Pax Romana*, (Weidenfeld and Nicolson, London, 2016).

Goldsworthy, Adrian, *The Complete Roman Army,* (Thames and Hudson, London, 2003).

Goldsworthy, Adrian, *Roman Warfare* (Phoenix, London, 2000).

Grant, Michael, *The Antonines*, (Routledge, London, 1994).

Grant, Michael, *The Roman Emperors*, (Phoenix, London, 1997).

Grigg, Eric, *Warfare and Raiding and Defence in Early Medieval Britain*, (Robert Hale, Marlborough 2018).

Halsall, Guy, *Barbarian Migrations and the Roman West 376-568*, (Cambridge University Press, Cambridge, 2014).

Hamilton, Walter, *Ammianus Marcellinus, The Later Roman Empire AD 354-378* (Penguin Books, London, 1986).

Hobbs, R. & Jackson, R., *Roman Britain,* (The British Museum Press, London, 2015).

Hoffmann, Birgitta, *The Roman Invasion of Britain, Archaeology versus History*, (Pen and Sword, Barnsley, 2013)

Hopkins, Keith and Beard, Mary, *The Colosseum*, (Profile Books, London, 2005).

Hughes, Ian, *Patricians and Emperors*, (Pen and Sword, Barnsley, 2015).

References

Kershaw, Stephen, *Barbarians, Rebellion and Resistance to Ancient Rome*, (Robinson, London, 2019).

Laycock, Stuart, *Britannia The Failed State,* (The History Press, Stroud, 2011).

Levick, Barbara, *Claudius*, (Routledge, Abingdon, 2013)

Levick, Barbara, *The Government of the Roman Empire*, (Routledge, London, 2000).

Levick, Barbara, *Vespasian*, (Routledge, Abingdon, 2019).

Livy, *The Early History of Rome*, (Penguin, Middlesex, 1960).

Mannix, Daniel, R., *Those About to Die*, (Granada Publishing, London, 1972).

Martial, *Epigrams With parallel Latin text (Oxford World's Classics)*, (Oxford University Press, Oxford, 2015).

McHugh, John, *The Emperor Commodus, God and Gladiator*, (Pen and Sword, Barnsley, 2015).

McLynn, Frank, *Marcus Aurelius, Warrior, Philosopher, Emperor*, (Vintage, London, 2010).

Milner, N, P, *Vegetius: Epitome of Military Science 2nd Ed* (Liverpool University Press, Liverpool, 2011).

Moffatt, Alistair, *The Wall, Rome's Greatest Frontier*, (Birlinn, Edinburgh, 2017).

Moorhead, Sam, and Stuttard, David, *The Romans who Shaped Britain*, (Thames and Hudson, London, 2016).

Nossov, Konstantin, *Gladiator, The Complete Guide to Ancient Rome's Bloody Fighters*, (Lyons Press, Guilford, 2011).

Ottaway, Peter, *Roman York*, (Tempus Books, Stroud, 2004).

Pearson, Andrew, *The Roman Shore Forts,* (The History Press, Stroud, 2010).

Penrose, Jane, *Rome and Her Enemies*, (Osprey Publishing, Oxford, 2005)

Pitassi, Michael, *The Roman Navy, Ships, Men and Warfare 350 BC – AD 475*, (Seaforth Publishing, Barnsley, 2012).

Plutarch, *Fall of the Roman Republic*, (Penguin, Middlesex, 1972).

Pollard, Nigel and Berry, Joanne, *The Complete Roman Legions*, (Thames and Hudson, London, 2015).

Richardson, John, *The Romans and the Antonine Wall of Scotland*, (Lulu.com, 2019)

Rivet, A.L.F., and Smith, Colin, *The Place-Names of Roman Britain,* (Batsford, London, 1982).

Rogan, John, *Roman Provincial Administration*, (Amberley Publishing, Stroud, 2011).

Sage, Michael, *Septimius Severus and the Roman Army*, (Pen and Sword, Barnsley, 2020).

Salway, Peter, *A History of Roman Britain,* (Oxford University Press, Oxford, 2001).

Scarre, Chris, *Chronicle of the Roman Emperors*, (Thames and Hudson, London, 2007).

Shadrake, Susanna, *The World of the Gladiator*, (Tempus, Stroud, 2005).

Shotter, David, *The Roman Frontier in Britain*, (Carnegie Publishing, Preston, 1996).

Southern, Patricia, *Roman Britain, A New History 55 BC – AD 450*, (Amberley Publishing, Stroud, 2013).

Southern, Patricia, *The Roman Army, A History 753 BC – AD 476*, (Amberley Publishing, Stroud, 2016).

Strauss, Barry, *The Spartacus War*, (Phoenix, London, 2010).

Suetonius, *The Life of the Caesars*, (Oxford University Press, Oxford, 2008).

Sullivan, Tony, *The Real Gladiator*, (Pen and Sword, Barnsley, 2022).

Summerton, Nick, *Greco-Roman Medicine,* (Pen and Sword, Barnsley, 2021).

Sumner, Graham, *Roman Military Dress*, (The History Press, Stroud, 2009).

Sumner, Graham, *Roman Warriors, The Paintings of Graham Sumner*, (Greenhill Books, Barnsley, 2022).

Symonds, Matthew, *Hadrian's Wall, Creating Division*, (Bloomsbury, London, 2021).

Syvanne, Ilkka, *Caracalla, A Military Biography*, (Pen and Sword, Barnsley, 2017).

Tacitus, *Agricola and Germania*, (Penguin Classics, London, 2009).

Tacitus, *The Histories*, (Oxford University Press, Oxford, 2008).

Taylor, Don, *Roman Empire at War*, (Pen and Sword, Barnsley, 2016).

Todd, Malcolm, *A Companion to Roman Britain*, (Blackwell Publishing, Malden, USA, 2007).

Tomlin, R.S.O., *Britannia Romana, Roman Inscriptions and Roman Britain*, (Oxbow Books, Oxford, 2018).

Travis, Hiliary and Travis, John, *Roman Body Armour*, (Amberley, Stroud, 2012).

References

Travis, Hiliary and Travis, John, *Roman Helmets*, (Amberley, Stroud, 2016).

Travis, Hiliary and Travis, John, *Roman Shields*, (Amberley, Stroud, 2016).

Wacher, John, The Towns of Roman Britain, (BCA, London, 1995).

Webb, Simon, *Life in Roman London,* (The History Press, Stroud, 2011).

Webster, Graham, *The Roman Invasion of Britain*, (Routledge, London 1993).

Webster, Graham, *The Roman Imperial Army*, (A & C Black, London, 1981).

ENDNOTES

Introduction

1. Elliott, 2016: 48

Chapter 1: The historical background

1. Beard, 2016: 58
2. Beard, 2016: 59
3. Beard, 2016: 56
4. Beard, 2016: 91
5. Beard, 2016: 218
6. McLynn, 2009: 13

Chapter 2: Vespasian's early life

1. Davenport, 2019: 8
2. Davenport, 2019: 37
3. Davenport, 2019: 135-9
4. Davenport, 2019: 16
5. Cassius Dio, book 59.10
6. Webster, 1981: 109
7. Milner, 2011: 72
8. Milner, 2011: 44
9. McLynn, 2009: 325
10. Webster, 1981: 146
11. Webster, 1981: 150

Chapter 3: The invasion of Britain

1. Goldsworthy, 2009: 337
2. Julius Caesar, Gallic Wars, book 4.25
3. Elliott, 2021: 43-4
4. Goldsworthy, 2009: 347
5. Elliott, 2021: 57
6. Elliott, 2021: 61
7. Suetonius, *De Vita Caesarum*, The Lives of the Twelve Caesars, Claudius
8. Grant, 1997: 30
9. Elliott, 2021: 67
10. Cassius Dio, *Historia Romana*, Roman History, 53.22
11. Cassius Dio, *Historia Romana*, Roman History 54.25
12. Suetonius, *De Vita Caesarum*, The Lives of the Twelve Caesars, Claudius 17
13. Strabo, Geography, 5.8
14. Levick, 2013: 167
15. Cassius Dio, book 60.19-23
16. Elliott, 2021: 80
17. Webster, 1993: 101
18. Caesar, Gallic Wars book 4.17-20
19. Webster, 1993: 101
20. Cassius Dio, book 60.21
21. Webster, 1993: 106
22. Strabo, Geography, Book 4, chapter 5.2
23. Caesar, Gallic Wars Book 5.9
24. Caesar, Gallic Wars Book 5.21
25. Collins, 2020: 23
26. Crummy, 1997: 11
27. Crummy, 1997: 13
28. Crummy, 1997: 15
29. Pliny the Elder, *Naturalis Historia*, Natural History, book 2.77
30. Tacitus Annals, 12.32
31. Wacher, 1995: 114-21
32. Tacitus, Annal, book 14.31

Chapter 4: Vespasian's campaign in southern Britain

1. Suetonius, The Life of Vespasian, 4.1
2. Wacher, 1995: 335
3. Wacher, 1995: 323
4. Webster, 1993: 108
5. Webster, 1993: 109-10
6. Tacitus Annals, book 14, chapters 34-37
7. Tacitus, *Life of Agricola*, chapter 30
8. Clarkson, 2019: 17
9. Webster, 1993: 109
10. Cassius Dio, book 49.29-31
11. Ammianus Book 23.4
12. Goldsworthy, 2003: 244
13. Josephus, The Jewish War, Book III chapter 7
14. Procopius, Gothic war, chapter XXI
15. Procopius, Gothic war, chapter XXIII
16. Milner, 2011: 10
17. Milner, 2011: 24 & 80-81
18. Breeze, 208: 39
19. Webster, 1985: 119
20. Cunliffe, 2013: 239-49
21. Cunliffe, 2013: 303-4
22. Strabo, *Geographica*, book 4 chapter 5
23. Julius Caesar, Gallic War books 4 and 5
24. Tacitus, *De vita Julii Agricolae*, The Life of Agricola
25. https://www.warhistoryonline.com/ancient-history/archers-roman-army.html
26. Underwood, 1999: 25
27. Grigg, 2018: 72

Chapter 5: The fall and rise of Vespasian's career

1. Cassius Dio Book 61.13.5
2. Grant, 1997: 35
3. Levick, 2017: 37

4. Tacitus, The Histories 5.16
5. https://www.livius.org/articles/place/xanten/xanten-victory-monument/

Chapter 6: The Colosseum, Vespasian's Greatest Monument

1. Hopkins and Beard, 2005: 2
2. Hopkins and Beard, 2011: 109
3. Hopkins and Beard, 2011: 54
4. Nossov, 2009: 12
5. Nossov, 2009: 14
6. Epplett, 2020: 3
7. Epplett, 2020: 10
8. Nossov, 2009: 16-7
9. Hopkins and Beard, 2011: 98
10. Nossov, 2009: 15
11. Nossov, 2009: 20
12. Epplett, 2020: 64
13. Epplett, 2020: 36
14. Epplett, 2020: 70
15. Epplett, 2020:73-4
16. Epplett, 2020: 85-6
17. Hopkins and Beard, 2011: 42
18. Epplett, 2020: 34
19. Nossov, 2009: 32
20. Nossov, 2009: 33
21. Hopkins and Beard, 2011: 45
22. Epplett, 2020: 31
23. Epplett, 2020: 51
24. Nossov, 2009: 38
25. Nossov, 2009: 38
26. Hopkins and Beard, 2011: 51
27. Hopkins and Beard, 2011: 55
28. Epplett, 2020: xii
29. Nossov, 2009: 45
30. Bishop, 2017: 84-98

31. Nossov, 2009: 71
32. Epplett, 2020: xii
33. Shadrake, 2005: 85
34. Hopkins and Beard, 2011: 77
35. Shadrake, 2005: 79
36. Hopkins and Beard, 2011: 86-9
37. Shadrake, 2005: 95
38. Shadrake, 2005: 95
39. Hopkins and Beard, 2011: 85
40. Epplett, 2020: 79
41. Hopkins and Beard, 2011: 90-4
42. Shadrake, 2005: 91
43. Hopkins and Beard, 2011: 49
44. Martial, *de spectaculis*, 29
45. Epplett, 2020: 98
46. Epplett, 2020: 99
47. Hopkins and Beard, 2011: 56
48. Epplett, 2020: 31
49. Epplett, 2020: 45
50. Epplett, 2020: 64
51. Epplett, 2020: 32
52. Epplett, 2020: 60-1
53. Epplett, 2020: 104
54. Epplett, 2020: 23
55. Hopkins and Beard, 2011: 60
56. Epplett, 2020: 60
57. Hopkins and Beard, 2011: 43
58. Epplett, 2020: 33

Chapter 7: Emperor

1. Levick, 2019: 78
2. Levick, 2019: 167
3. Josephus, book 7.3
4. Birley, 2005: 65
5. Ottaway, 2004: 26

6. Ottaway, 2004: 31
7. Ottaway, 2004: 24
8. Elliott, 2021: 67
9. Elliott, 2021: 145-8
10. Birley, 2005: 228-30
11. Elliott, 2021: 64
12. Levick, 2019: 79
13. Levick, 2019: 88
14. Levick, 2019: 232
15. Levick, 2019: 236-7
16. Levick, 2019: 236

Chapter 8: Legacy

1. Suetonius, The life of Titus
2. Cassius Dio, book 65.25
3. Hopkins and Beard, 2011: 43
4. Cassius Dio, book 66.26

INDEX